B4

The Thai And I

The Thai And I

Living In The Thai Countryside

Håkan Kolmodin

Published and Distributed by
Asia Books Co. Ltd.,
5 Sukhumvit Road Soi 61,
PO Box 40,
Bangkok 10110,
Thailand.
Tel: (66) 0-2715-9000 ext. 3202–4
Fax: (66) 0-2714-2799
E-mail: information@asiabooks.com
Website: www.asiabooks.com

 Illustrations by Prawit Mongkolnawarat.

Typeset by COMSET Limited Partnership.
Printed in Thailand.

ISBN 974-8303-89-6

Contents

Prologue

My wife and I have lived and worked in rural Thailand for over ten years, and have experienced its society from the inside—something which most tourists don't get a chance to do. Our time in the Thai countryside has also given us an entirely different view of Thailand from that of other foreigners who work for big international companies and live in Bangkok.

It can be difficult for a foreigner to learn about Thai society. You sometimes feel totally lost in unknown territory. The purpose of this book is to describe Thailand in a way that goes beyond the beautiful backdrop found in tourist guides.

Thailand is going through a dramatic transformation, and we've been in the middle of the action. A traditional agricultural society is dissolving and a new order is evolving from the chaos. We have often found it hard to understand some things because we don't speak Thai fluently, but I've tried to distil my experiences to give an introduction to the modern Thailand that is now emerging. This book may provide some guidance to others who are trying to find their way in this country, and help them to avoid the mistakes that we have made.

We would like to thank all our Thai friends who have helped us adjust to life here and have overlooked our strange customs. Thanks to their help, we have acquired a certain insight into Thai society. Still, I may have misunderstood some of the things that I have tried to describe here, and if so, I sincerely apologize.

Håkan Kolmodin,
Prachin Buri, 2005

1. New Challenges

It was a Saturday evening in December and the next day was the fourth Sunday in Advent. The long winter night had fallen on our neighbourhood in Falun in the middle of Sweden, but frost on the lawns reflected scattered light. Our children were home from their respective universities to spend Christmas with Mum and Dad.

The gingerbread dough had been kept in the cellar overnight and it was now time for the father of the house to attend to his most important Christmas duty. Would the dough be supple enough this year? Or would the children have to endure their father's grumbling about it being too tough to transform into gingerbread biscuits and the traditional gingerbread house? They would naturally have to sample the dough, and so would the house cat, who had slipped into the kitchen where the heat from the oven was starting to spread. Christmas music played softly in this haven of familiar traditions.

The phone had been ringing regularly as the kids' friends kept calling to plan Christmas parties. Suddenly my son's voice boomed over the cosy family gathering. "Dad, some guy called Hans wants to talk to you!"

From that moment, nothing would be the same. Our traditionally rich Swedish life would be torn away and replaced by a new one on the other side of the world.

What thoughts enter your head when someone interrupts you in the middle of baking Christmas gingerbread and asks if you want to change jobs and move to a small village in Thailand to build a new paper-mill? The answer is that an agony of indecision sets in. Where exactly was this place? We weren't much wiser after a visit to the city library, but Thailand certainly looked inviting as we flicked through picture books showing temples, sun-drenched beaches, and pretty girls. My wife Gunilla and I had all sorts of questions. What were we to do with our house, which we had so tirelessly renovated over fifteen years? How would we stay in touch with our children from the other side of the world? Who would look after the cat? And if Gunilla quit her job as a schoolteacher, how would she occupy herself out in the remote rice fields?

Through sleepless nights we went through the pros and cons, over and over again until our stomachs felt like they were full of fluttering tropical butterflies. Our whole existence, built around traditions and security, would have to be uprooted.

But what made it so enticing to pack up and leave home for the unknown? Both Gunilla and I felt that we had reached a stage of our lives when we needed something new. After 25 years of raising kids, we were now mostly on our own in the house, with no one but the old cat pattering around. We were both past fifty and felt we were trundling down an uneventful path to retirement. When the offer from Thailand tumbled down into the Christmas gingerbread dough, we eventually succumbed to this opportunity to try something new.

One day, a couple of months later, a thick express-delivery envelope arrived with an employment contract. What was I about to sign? With a palpable sense of fate, I affixed my name next to the peculiarly long name of the Thai CEO. After that, we waited. How could we explain to friends and family that we were leaving our nice house and good jobs to venture out into the unknown? These were some of their reactions:

"You're out of your minds, quitting your perfectly good jobs!"

"But you've been living here for so many years!"

"Can the children really take care of themselves?"

"What about the house that you've put so much effort into?"

"What do your parents have to say about this jaunt of yours?"

"How will you be able to handle the climate?"

"You'll have to get vaccinations for all those dangerous tropical diseases!"

Of course, a really hectic period followed. Stuff we had accumulated over half a lifetime had to be cleaned out and stowed away. Finally, we stood in front of our home with one big suitcase each, waiting for the taxi to take us to the airport.

What had we got ourselves into?

☙❦

When we landed at Bangkok's Don Muang Airport, an incredibly humid heat struck us in the face when we left the cabin. It felt like walking into a greenhouse. Sweat blurred our vision and dripped down our backs. We felt a bit lost when we lined up at Immigration to get our passports stamped. We couldn't read the signs, written in weird squiggles, although one urgent situation that arose at the luggage claim was easily solved: just like the toilet signs in Sweden, men wore trousers

and women skirts, and we could ignore the incomprehensible letters for the time being.

As we soon learned at the airport, it is hard for a foreigner to hide among the Thais. There's the obvious matter of height. Gunilla often complained of her short stature in Sweden, always having to look up to everyone, resenting having to ask for help to get kitchen utensils from the top shelves. But now, in the middle of a crowd, she looked over the heads of almost everyone. Most of the people were very petite. Gunilla looked at the policemen, who inspired respect in their trim uniforms. Upon their hips hung large-calibre pistols and impressive cartridge-belts, resembling sheriffs of the Wild West. The comparison ended, though, as their shoulders were only as wide as their hips.

We found our luggage and the driver who was going to take us to our new home in the Thai countryside. Even if most things felt foreign, we soon felt welcome in this exotic place.

☙❧

At the end of World War II, Thailand was still a traditional agricultural society, with three-quarters of its land mass covered by tropical forest. Over the next three decades, the Thais made a massive investment in agriculture: clearing and cultivating new land, digging irrigation canals. The forests yielded valuable tropical hardwoods, much sought after on

the world market, which only added to rapid deforestation. Today, less than 25 percent of Thailand is covered by forest land, which is now officially protected though still victim to ruthless illegal loggers.

The next phase of Thai economic development took place during the 1980s and early 90s when Thailand sought to build an export industry, and rural people flooded into the cities, Bangkok being by far the most powerful magnet. The capital quickly burgeoned into a monster of over 10 million, suffering from the growing pains of pollution, massive traffic jams, and environmental degradation.

To reduce the pressure on Bangkok, the government encouraged industry to locate outside the city, offering various kinds of incentives to companies that established themselves in rural areas. Industrial zones were created with access to the necessary infrastructure. My new job was going to be at one of these industrial compounds in the Thai countryside. Our multinational team of experts was to construct, start up, and operate a new paper-mill.

Just like in the old Swedish steel industry, we lived closely together and our tasks created a sense of community and friendship among us. The atmosphere seemed comparable to that at the start of the Swedish industrial era in the 1600s, when King Charles IX invited skilled craftsmen from Wallonia, in present-day Belgium, to erect ironworks close to the rich iron-ore mines in Dannemora. The set-up that we saw in the Thai countryside resembled the layout of the ironworks in the Swedish county of Uppland, but in Thailand the manor house was represented by a modern hotel with spacious arcades and lotus ponds. It was here that we were temporarily accomodated while our company houses were under construction. Upper management lived in the houses closest to the hotel; workers furthest away. The size of one's house wasn't determined by need but by rank. The company built a small supermarket, and electricity came from the mill's power plant. The Swedish ironworks had a proprietor who reigned supreme. The Thai equivalent was the company's executive director, who was also the majority shareholder.

But not everything in Thailand resembles a well-designed and efficient Swedish industrial site. The first and perhaps most obvious difference is that all Thai employees are expected to wear the company's safari-suit uniform. A Swedish policewoman who was on holiday came to visit us

at the mill and thought that we looked like a bunch of prisoners. But the uniform is very practical and can even be worn to attend dinner with foreign guests—and weddings and funerals, too. You never have to worry about what to wear if invited to some official party.

This new industrial community on the plains of Thailand was completely surrounded by a traditional agricultural society. All around the mill stretched fields of tapioca and straight-lined plantations of eucalyptus trees. A couple of kilometres away, in the midst of the rice paddies, stood a small village with its Buddhist temple and school, where Gunilla eventually came to assist with the fifty children at the kindergarten. Narrow gravel roads lined with bamboo and brushwood meandered through the fields. Small, simple farmhouses nestled in the shade of banana, mango, and papaya trees.

In the beginning it was hard for a Swedish housewife to find what she needed for everyday life in the Thai countryside. When we arrived at this pioneer community, the construction had already been going on for a year. Heavy monsoon rains left a layer of mud over the whole neighbourhood. There wasn't much but muddy building sites, and we had to go to nearby villages to purchase necessities.

The district capital, Srimahapot, was fifteen kilometres away, a typical little Thai provincial town with low-rise wooden houses. A big market-place displayed fresh produce, small shops along the main street sold all kinds of merchandise, but it wasn't easy to find everything that we needed. Many expeditions were made, and we eventually muddled through.

2. A Different World

Behind the façade of Western influence in Thailand, there's another world here that is not easily described. Thai society displays cultural traits that can confuse and perplex Westerners, especially those trying to do business. Modern communications have brought this part of the world closer to us, but many mysteries still remain.

Even before the modern 'blessings' of the Western world were adopted by the Thais, many different peoples lived here in a comparatively frictionless atmosphere of understanding. The Chinese especially have long been an established minority who now dominate the business and political world.

Thailand has shown a big interest in the outside world since the reign of King Mongkut (r. 1851-1868). His son, Chulalongkorn (1853-1910),

made study trips to India and Indonesia and, later in his own reign (1868-1910), travelled extensively on state visits to Europe. Initial Western influences on Thai society were mainly technological and administrative. Even though the absolute monarchy was abolished in 1932 and 'free elections' are held, the Western perception of democracy has never really taken root here and, in essence, Thailand remains a feudal system, with local 'fiefdoms' dominated by influential businessmen and politicians.

Today, the tourism industry and the influence of the media, especially television, has quickened the development of a consumer society. Old family traditions are breaking up, and a youth culture of individualism thrives. The manufacturing industry bestows economic opportunities in a materialistic environment beyond the Buddhist ideals of spiritual growth through liberation from worldly concerns.

The West is far from being a homogenous cultural unity. Nevertheless, we Westerners have many values in common that make us a uniform group in comparison to the subtle nuances of the social order that reigns in Thailand. And, indeed, the Thai people lump all Caucasians together as *farangs* (there are similar-sounding words throughout the East going back to the Franks of the Crusades) no matter where we're from.

The Judeo-Christian cultural heritage is almost part of our genes. The Ten Commandments still represent the foundation of Western legislation and moral concepts. In the West, the democratic system is widely accepted, and general elections supposedly express the will of the people. The judicial system is based on legislation that warrants a uniform administration of justice regardless of birth or economic status. In reality, this is most definitely not the case in Thailand. Exceptions can, of course, be found to these ideals, but this cultural heritage characterizes the foreigner in his or her relations to the surrounding world.

Usually, Westerners expect mutual trust and openness. Honesty is a concept of honour that implies that agreements entered into should be kept. Foreigners rely on laws being followed and contracts being completed with no additional payments swapping hands. Once in a while the Westerner also wants a long holiday with his family. This behaviour and these expectations make the foreigner stand out like a strange bird in Thailand.

☙❦❧

Following an initial period of excitement, our lives returned to normal—and a new thought became more and more obvious: it wasn't

Thailand that was different, but we were the foreign creatures in this, our new home. We were the "aliens" according to the official definition on the signs at the passport counter, and in everyday life we were *farangs*—the strange people from the West.

In the countryside we became more and more conscious of ourselves. We heard how people would talk about us behind our backs, the word *farang* occurring again and again. Mothers bent down to their children and pointed us out: the bizarre creatures whose pointy nosed heads towered over the throng in the market-place. We must indeed have appeared very unusual. Our perception opened up more and more, and we started to see ourselves through the eyes of a Thai. We were the water buffaloes in the vegetable patch.

On our visits to Bangkok, where foreigners are a more common part of the street scene, we soon realized how various Thai perceptions have come about. Sure enough, it is hot in Bangkok and the visitor wants to wear casual clothes on holiday, but one can't blame the Thais for sniggering and whispering '*farang*' when the oversized tourist walks nonchalantly along the city pavements dressed in shorts and singlet (instances of bikinis and other swimwear are not unknown), with camera around neck and big belly flopping atop a bumbag. The tourist has also

just spent a week by the sea and his corpulent body has been burned lobster red. Not a pretty sight for the Thais.

It is not only physical appearance that distinguishes the foreigner. When he opens his mouth to talk, it can sound like a tropical thunderstorm to the normally soft-spoken Thais. The difficulties in communication arise from both parties. A feeling of insecurity in speaking to a foreigner can make a Thai lower his voice even further. The foreigner reacts to a situation like this by raising his voice to show that he doesn't understand what is being said, or to make his point—which only makes the Thai more uncomfortable. In Thai culture it is a virtue to not raise one's voice or to show irritation.

To the Thais there are two expressions central to social etiquette and social interaction that can be easily misinterpreted by a foreigner: 'cool heart' and 'hot heart.' The foreigner considers a warm heart a virtue, and that people with cold hearts are insensitive. He is thus totally at odds to the Thai way of thinking, at least in terms of word definitions. A Thai person has, from early childhood, been brought up not to show any strong emotions, especially anger. The meaning of the Thai expression *jai ron* (literally 'heart hot') does not indicate 'warm-heartedness'; it is more akin to the English expression 'hot-tempered.' Similarly, the Thai expression *jai yen* (literally 'heart cool') is akin to the English 'keeping one's cool,' or being even tempered, and does not mean 'cold-heartedness.' Thus the confusion.

Some forms of behaviour that the foreigner would consider an obvious breach of etiquette are, on the other hand, totally acceptable to Thais—like picking one's nose in public. I find it hard to act naturally when my otherwise exquisitely mannered Thai assistant, during a conversation, drills a finger up her nose, oblivious to all and everyone around her.

An American project engineer once told me how he had been confronted with Thai sensibilities for the first time. The schedule for construction of the mill had gone off track and Dick, the pragmatic American, wanted to have a talk to the Thai project manager, Viroj. Dick sought out the Thai in his office and sat down opposite him to list all the obstacles that were holding up construction.

Dick might have built up some adrenalin before he started the conversation and his tone of voice was not properly subdued. Viroj put on a poker face right from the start and didn't show the least sign of understanding that the Thai organization wasn't working adequately. In a situation like this, a foreigner reacts instinctively and raises his voice to give more emphasis to his views. A Thai hides what he actually feels deep down inside.

Viroj leaned back in his chair and looked up at the ceiling. His nose started to itch and he pulled out two inhaler tubes. He drilled, with emphasis, one tube into each nostril, so that he resembled a walrus.

Dick was now close to exploding and raised his voice even more. At this point, Viroj lowered his eyes from the ceiling, looked at Dick straight in the eye and, with the inhalers still sticking out of his nose, said in a low, composed voice, "I don't like your manners." At that point, Dick found it best to remove himself from the room and try to cool down his unsuitably 'hot heart.'

3. Language Barriers

Tourists get a very pleasant impression upon their first contact with Thai people. They are greeted with generous smiles and are treated kindly, even when they show irritation when something isn't working out as expected. Watch, for instance, the receptionist at a Thai hotel when a discontented and over-excited foreigner loudly berates her about how bad the service is. After receiving all the complaints in perfect self-control, the receptionist answers with a smile, 'No problem!'

It is easy to get the impression that the Thais are an incredibly friendly people, radiating harmony. There is probably some truth in that, but a lot of the smiling has to do with the way Thai people communicate. Thais generally don't wave their hands to shout 'hi'; instead they greet each other with a wide smile. They generally keep a modulated tone in con-

versation and don't often raise their voices to emphasize the importance of what they're saying. As mentioned, it is considered very inappropriate to show irritation or anger, and Thai people get very embarrassed when a Westerner gives vent to his feelings. Faced with such a scene, Thais will simply smile or find some way to avoid the situation.

The language, however, imposes the greatest limits when a foreigner wants to take relations one step further. Thais, though, have a certain imagination and will generally make an effort to understand a foreigner who is trying to master their tongue. They'll certainly appreciate the effort, no matter how bad your Thai. Thais will subject a foreigner to a language test such as '*Mai mai mai, mai*?' which means 'Does new silk burn?' and laugh heartily, but not mockingly, at your clumsy attempts to catch the right tones.

If the foreigner finds it difficult to learn Thai, the difficulties are no less the other way. Concepts that Westerners find very natural don't exist in the Thai language, and many English-language constructions are tricky for Thais.

Avoid negative questions, for instance. If you ask a Thai, 'Don't you understand this?' he will reply 'Yes,' meaning he acknowledges your question and doesn't understand it. But some Thais may have learned how to reply in the English manner, so you can never be totally sure how to interpret such an answer. A good piece of advice is simply to avoid ambiguous questions. Beyond this, a Thai finds it hard to admit that he has not understood your instructions in English. So it's important to read facial expressions and, if in doubt, explain everything once more, slowly.

Simple things such as using different greetings for different times of the day can lead to comical situations. Our office maid, who delivers mail to my office twice a day, was curious to learn some English phrases. She had learned to say 'Good morning, sir,' but used this greeting in the afternoons, too. One afternoon I spent some time teaching her to say 'Good afternoon, sir,' and I felt like Professor Higgins in "Pygmalion." When she entered my office the next morning, she put on her biggest smile and said, "Good afternoon, sir!"

In the Bangkok business world and the big tourist resorts, you can usually get by using English, but not in the rest of Thailand. Even young people with university degrees can't handle a simple phrase or description in English. Reading skills are better, since they learn some English in junior school. Even though Thai children start learning the language in their first grade, the English comprehension of rural teachers is very rudimentary and most children who leave school after nine years can't say much more than 'Hello, sir' and 'Thank you, sir,' saying these phrases to both men and women.

My Swedish colleague Arne found himself in an embarrassing situation one evening. It happened early in our stay when we were still quartered in the half-finished hotel, waiting for our houses to be completed. Arne's family had returned to Sweden after their summer visit and he felt a bit abandoned. There was a cautious knock on the door

and when Arne opened it, a small Thai girl was standing in the hallway. With eyelids demurely downcast, she said in a whisper, "You lonely?" Arne, quickly assessing the situation, said, "I'm alone but not lonely." The maid repeated her question: "You laundry?" She had just failed to pronounce the 'R' sound in the word.

Of course, I made my own mistakes. In the mornings when I met my office staff, I would greet them with 'Good morning' or the general Thai phrase, '*Sawatdee khrap.*' I seldom received a reply, so I considered the Thais to be either sleepy or impolite. One morning our secretary came up to me and asked whether I had any trouble, because the office girls thought I looked so serious when I said 'Good morning.' What I said as I came in the door each morning apparently didn't matter much; the important thing was my facial expression. A big generous smile got a totally different reception and I had to start practicing my 'good morning smile' in the mirror each day before I went to the mill.

Language was indeed a barrier for me, and I often had to ask for help to convey my instructions to the staff. Learning how to cope in everyday situations with an elementary knowledge in Thai is one thing; participating in technical discussions is a whole different matter. Meetings took on an agenda of their own, with lively side-translations around the table.

Lek, the sales manager, struggled courageously with the English language, but she had great difficulty in understanding Bob, a production engineer from Mississippi, who spoke with a deep southern accent. Eventually she managed to grasp a few words here and there, so Bob improvised a language test:

"We are starting to understand each other very well now, aren't we?"

"Yes, yes."

"So now you have no difficulties in understanding me?"

"Yes, yes."

"And now you are ready to marry me?"

"Yes, yes."

"So it is all right, then, for me to go home and tell my wife to prepare for our wedding?"

"Yes, yes."

Bob burst out laughing and Lek, who realized she had understood nothing, giggled with embarrassment.

Thai culture demands that you don't trouble a person in a higher position of authority. Therefore you don't ask for explanations. Nor do you make any objections when asked to perform a task. Ask a Thai person if he can have some work done by tomorrow and he will answer 'No problem.' But almost certainly it won't be done. The idea is not to disappoint the boss but keep him happy as long as possible. Thus, Thais won't report problems or complications to their boss, but will try to sort out the situation as best they can before having to report. Positive reports put the boss in a good mood and create an atmosphere that might advance the subordinate's career.

A Westerner who works with Thais eventually comes to feel as if they are not part of the team. You may think that you have established good personal relations with your Thai colleagues, and you might socialize outside work at restaurants or on the golf course, but it is still hard to break through cultural barriers. This is partly because the Thai people find it difficult to explain what is going on. One reason is the language problem, the other is that they don't willingly talk about obstacles that can spoil one's day. Let the boss believe that everything is working as it's supposed to, and he will be happy.

4. Taste Sensations

Food plays a central role in everyday Thai life, and you find an incredibly wide range of dishes and delicacies wherever you go. On city streets, in local markets, out in the countryside, vendors stand behind their pushcarts cooking food from morning to late at night. Customers are served at small, rickety tables set up on the pavement, where cooking smells mix with the traffic exhaust. Many Thais never cook at home, they just go out into the street to eat. Employees buy plastic bags of their favourite dishes to bring along to the workplace. The price is cheap, so why not enjoy?

Meals are heavily spiced, with various chillies an important ingredient. Chilli fragrances from woks linger in the air, making the eyes of unwary foreigners sting and water. For a proper Thai meal, people gather in a group and order several different dishes that are placed in the middle of the table. A big scoop of rice is put on your plate, then everyone helps themselves, spooning up sauces and mixing them over the rice. You eat with a tablespoon in your right hand, a fork in your left. It is a very practical way of eating rice. Compare with the average Westerner who struggles, through ingrained convention, to spoon up his fried rice with a fork.

Most restaurants in the countryside don't have walls, so you are more or less dining outdoors. Dust inevitably settles as a thin film over everything, so it is customary to wipe your plate and cutlery with a napkin first. While we were still new to Thailand, we tried to learn about Thai cuisine, and sampled our way through restaurant menus. Unexpected taste sensations made sweat beads on our foreheads, but eventually we learned to order meals with balanced tastes. Four ingredients used in a Thai meal for proper balance are fish sauce for saltiness, lime for a sour tang, sugar for sweetness, and chilli for fire. Gunilla took a cooking course to learn how to prepare meat and vegetables in the Thai way, and to flavour dishes with herbs and chilli. The course took place in a traditional Thai teak house along one of the many canals that still cut through Bangkok's suburbs. Small boats loaded with fresh produce passed by just under the shade of the coconut palms where the lessons took place. Gunilla returned full of enthusiasm, and soon new and exciting fragrances were wafting through our home.

One day we invited a group of Thai friends to sample Gunilla's cooking skills. It probably felt a bit unfamiliar for the Thais to come around to a foreigner's home and sit down at a table laid out in the Swedish manner, with patterned Duni napkins decoratively placed on the plates. Our friends sat down expectantly and, to Gunilla's horror, took up their napkins to wipe their cutlery and plates. Gunilla maintained

her composure, though, and served up the dishes to be sampled. One guest rose, took up one of the big communal bowls, and went into the kitchen. Exploring our selection of spices, he mixed in more fish sauce, lime, and chillies. Then he returned to the table, content with a much more authentically Thai dish.

Rice is the staple of a Thai meal and to 'eat' in the Thai language, *kin khao*, is 'to consume rice.' So ingrained is rice in Thai culture that when friends meet casually or talk on the phone, the second question asked, after the initial greeting, is almost inevitably *kin khao reua yang*? ('Have you eaten yet?') A Thai dinner must include a big scoop of rice, otherwise the meal is not complete and your stomach is not really full. This is a serious issue for Thais, and many foreigners simply do not understand when their Thai friends hesitate for a moment when being invited to dinner in an Italian restaurant. Food without rice? It's a tough situation.

Traditionally in the countryside, people go to the rice dealer, pick their preferred type of rice, and have it scooped up from a big burlap sack. But in this way you also get small stowaways, and our rice bag often swarmed with tiny creeping creatures. Gunilla, devoted to the Swedish Board of Consumer Affairs, naturally couldn't accept these 'domestic' animals and returned with our sack to the rice seller to complain. The dealer looked blankly down at the rice bag, then up at Gunilla, smiled his best smile and replied with the standard Thai phrase, "No problem, no problem!" Gunilla wasn't convinced, whereupon the rice dealer added, "No problem, no hard bones!" Ever since then, Gunilla has bought rice in sealed plastic bags in the Western-style supermarkets that are now appearing in the countryside.

༄

Shortly after Gunilla and I had established ourselves in our house (see "At Home In Thailand") in the Thai countryside, our eating habits were scrutinized by the local children. We have a baking oven in our kitchen, and the children found that watching the bread rise in the oven was just as exciting as an action film on TV. One morning a young girl curiously watched us having breakfast, and after a while she ran back home to tell her grandmother about our strange habits. We later heard that the girl, with surprise in her voice, had reported that we did not even have rice for breakfast.

I have travelled to different countries with Thai colleagues on a number of occasions, and it always ends the same way. We have to find a Thai restaurant in order to avoid a serious case of malnutrition before returning to Thailand. Luckily, Thai cuisine is now popular in many countries, and there are fewer difficulties for Thai people travelling abroad.

The first time I travelled with one of my Thai assistants to Europe, we arrived late in the evening and, before retiring, we agreed to meet for breakfast in the hotel coffee shop. In the morning I could not find her in the coffee shop, but assumed that she had got up early, as most Thais do, and already had her breakfast. Later, when we were about to leave the hotel, I asked the young lady what she had for breakfast, but she gave me a very vague answer. After a while she admitted that when she entered the coffee shop early in the morning, the smell of freshly brewed coffee and fresh-made bread had made her feel sick. Instead she had sneaked out from the hotel and found a convenience store around the corner, where she bought a cup of Oriental instant noodles, which she consumed cold.

Next morning we had breakfast together and I tried to find something from the hotel buffet that a Thai might consider for breakfast. I scooped up some oatmeal porridge on a plate, put some blueberry jam on the top, and poured some milk around. I thought this would be a good substitute for *khao tom* (rice soup), which is the standard breakfast for most Thais. Well, the Thai girl had good manners and, sitting by my side, could not do anything else but finish her dish. She obviously didn't enjoy my improvised breakfast, but at least she was well fed before we started our working day.

The instant noodles, which can easily be heated in a microwave oven, are something of a survival kit for many Thais travelling abroad. A friend

working for an international telecommunications company told me about his experiences in a multicultural project team during a couple of months in Italy. The project was run in parallel in a number of countries, and a co-ordination team was formed in Italy with representatives from several of the countries involved. The co-ordination team worked hard, and in the evening most of the members went out to experience Italian food under the guidance of their local colleagues. But one team member did not join in the evening meals. The Thai representative had brought with him from Thailand one suitcase full of instant noodles. In the evening he preferred to stay in his room, where he could heat up the noodles in the microwave oven, instead of sampling the odd-tasting Italian cuisine.

Business travelling in China has been an exciting experience for me, and Chinese hospitality includes banquets with tables over-laden with all sorts of strange dishes, such as jellyfish, with its very strange texture. To a Western foreigner, many of the dishes look very dubious, but my Thai colleagues never seem to be fazed, and without hesitation sample the delicacies from the plates with their chopsticks. As the evening progresses, when dish number twenty has been put on the table and there is still no sign of any rice, the Thai guests around the table start to look worried. At last, one of them will pluck up the courage and politely ask the Chinese host if it would be possible to have some rice—without which, the meal would not seem complete. After all, it would not be possible to have good night's rest without a smooth layer of rice on top of all the strange creatures consumed during the evening.

As a Swede, I consider the potato a necessity of life and, luckily, potatoes are an ingredient in some Thai dishes. After some searching around, we found a vendor at a local market who had enormous potatoes. Other women soon discovered that the foreigners from the mill made up a ravenous new market for potatoes. 'Potato' in Thai is *man farang*, which loosely translates as 'foreign root.'

A visit to a local Thai food market, with all the exotic things on offer, gives the Westerner a marvelous sensory experience. Odours from aromatic spices, fermented fish, and freshly slaughtered meat hits you when you enter the shade of the market's roof. Flapping fish, jumping frogs, and crawling turtles are kept in big tubs. The fumes of barbecued delicacies such as squid, chicken's feet, and pig's trotters lay dense over the market-place. For the true gourmet, there are roasted grasshoppers or caterpillars.

Food-handling standards in Thailand are different to what a European is accustomed to. Pieces of meat are often displayed on wooden counters all day long, and the vendors try as best they can to keep the flies away. Shellfish, which we in Sweden handle with the strictest hygiene, are kept in tubs and the customers scoop up mussels or shrimps to put in their pot later without any concerns. However, seldom do you hear about anyone getting an upset stomach because of bad food. Fish and shellfish are kept alive or are delivered daily, and livestock slaughter takes place before dawn so that the meat doesn't have time to go bad during the day.

It is mostly pork that is sold at the market, and a standard price is valid for all pieces, so you have to arrive early if you want the more attractive cuts. Butchering is done on top of the counters, where the vendors sit on their heels, barefoot, working the knives. At our closest market-place, one girl's technique of cutting up meat was a bit special, but practical. When she was about to divide some spare ribs, she fixed the meat between her toes, which left both hands free for wielding the knife.

Fresh vegetables and herbal plants are displayed in big piles. Basil, mint, lemon grass, coriander, and many kinds of chilli are used to add flavour to Thai dishes and are staples in any Thai market. Chillies are also made into pastes with other spices and displayed in big bowls. These pastes vary in strength. Red, green, and yellow chilli pastes are used for cooking a group of curry dishes that the Thais call *gaeng*. I would rather describe them as 'chilli stews' made with chicken, pork, or fish. You should be careful with these hot dishes and eat a lot of rice to soak up the chilli oils and cool the palate. Drinking water will only spread the fire around the rest of your mouth.

Thais nibble snacks throughout the day, and there is always something to eat at the workplace. Small bowls and food parcels are scattered on office desks, work counters, and control panels. You can hardly open a desk drawer or a tool cupboard without finding crockery and cutlery just waiting to be used. As soon as there is a break, it's time for food.

One hot and humid day in the mill, Robert, a Swedish production engineer, was supervising a group of Thai operators. During a break, they gathered in the air-conditioned control room to recuperate. The Thais pulled out their food bowls and opened their plastic bags of rice and curry. Robert pulled a *snus* box from his pocket and stuck a big

pinch under his upper lip. This, of course, aroused curiosity, and one of the operators asked him what kind of strange candy this was. Robert explained that it was a sort of tobacco, and the Thai asked for a sample. Following Robert, he cautiously put a pinch under his lip. At first he looked thoughtful, but eventually a smile spread across his face. He started to hum a song and threw a bunch of work forms into the air. Then he staggered about drunkenly before falling unconscious to the floor. Roaring with laughter, his mates hauled him outside and hosed him down. After a while, he came to. He was deposited in a corner where he spent the rest of the shift singing to himself. At the end of the day, he had recovered enough to get himself home.

In comparison to a pinch of *snus*, you really have to view Thai chilli dishes as mere baby food.

5. Tropical Slumber

Newcomers to Thailand are sometimes struck by an unexpected fatigue in the evenings, and believe that this is just jet lag. But it is a completely natural tiredness that has to do with the climate—something that even the Thais are affected by. It may appear at first sight to be a sign of general laziness when people are sleeping during the most improbable occasions and in the most incredible places. However, when you live in constant humid heat, you realize that sleep is something you can't deny—and Thai people have an innate ability to sleep under almost unimaginable circumstances.

Away from the hectic lifestyle in Bangkok and the tourist resorts, bed times are usually early. If you go out for dinner with Thai friends in the countryside, you don't have to fear any late nights. By the time the

clock strikes 9:00, guests start to bat their eyelids sleepily and glance at their watches.

A survey published in a Bangkok paper asked adolescents about their spare-time activities. The most popular activity was to browse in shopping malls; the second was to sleep. When I first asked my co-workers about their weekend plans, I was surprised when they told me that they were going home to sleep. I was naturally expecting them to tell me about their favourite sports or pastimes, or visiting their parents, but to a young Thai, a weekend with lots of sleep is time well spent.

Working in a tropical thirty-degree climate is tiring. The need to sleep applies not only to manual labourers but to office workers, as well. At our mill's administration department, office girls work at small desks lined up in rows. Each desk is provided with three drawers—and their contents reflect their owners' priorities. The top drawer contains make-up, and the work day starts with a few minutes in the mirror. The middle drawer contains bowls and plates and cutlery so that they are able to snack all day. The bottom drawer, bigger than the other two, is used to store that all-important item: a pillow. While working, the girls put their pillow behind their backs for support, or sit on it to get extra height, but when the lunch break comes, they place the pillow on their desk, plop their heads down, and instantly fall into a deep sleep. Tranquillity descends upon the office.

In the local market, vendors have to protect themselves and their produce as best they can from the broiling sun. They erect big parasols

or tarpaulin 'roofs' over their stalls. For a permanent market, a shed with a roof of corrugated sheet metal comes into play. But it still gets very hot, and the lady vendors, who sit in their booths all day from early morning, will curl up like cats amongst their fruit and veg baskets, laying their head comfortably among the cabbages and sticking their feet into a pile of pineapples. If anyone stops at their stall to pick among their wares, they lift up a lazy eyelid like a napping watchdog.

During the hot, dry season, when the sun is merciless, the need for sleep becomes even greater. At the village schools where Gunilla works, there is no air-conditioning, only ceiling fans and big, open-shuttered windows. Fans stand in front of the teacher's desk, but Gunilla will often see a teacher overcome with the heat, stretched over her desk, sound asleep in the fan's breeze, while her pupils unconcernedly continue with writing exercises. For the children, it is totally natural for the teacher to be taking a nap.

Obviously, physical work is more demanding. On building sites you see what manual labour in a tropical climate really means. During the construction of the mill, a small building had to be erected to store some equipment. Sven, the Swedish construction manager, negotiated with a Thai contractor for its construction. Both parties agreed on the size of the workforce and the daily salary, estimating that twenty labourers would be needed during the month set aside for the job. When work started, Sven found that the size of the workforce didn't match the contract. There were significantly more than twenty workers on site, and many lay asleep in the shade. When Sven brought this up with the site foreman, he received the

standard Thai reply: "No problem." It transpired that Sven didn't have to pay more than what was agreed upon, and the sleeping contingent were not a problem either, since there were always twenty men at work. The sleepers were an unofficial reserve force in the form of friends and relatives who agreed to share the day's salary. In this way the workers could recuperate and sleep for a while during the day without anyone thinking

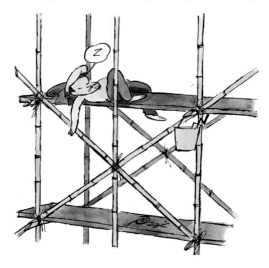

it amiss, and without the schedule being disrupted. And construction continued after sunset when it was a bit cooler.

The Thai ability to go to sleep in the noisiest, strangest, and most uncomfortable positions can be amazing. During the end phase of our mill construction, it was hard for the workers to find a good place to sleep. One day, I saw a man lying stretched out, his shirt rolled under his head, on a wooden plank on rickety bamboo scaffolding ten metres above the concrete floor. With his arms and legs dangling from each side of the plank, he looked like a panther napping on a branch in the jungle.

On the cramped mill floor, an electrician devised a novel method for his lunch nap. He found a plank and pushed it halfway into an electrical switchboard cabinet. On this board, with half his body inside the cabinet, the man was sound asleep

with unconnected electrical cables hanging down over his face.

A painter was standing on a ladder, about to give a bathroom its last lick of paint, when he was overwhelmed by an urgent need to wrap himself in the arms of Morpheus. With a paint bucket in one hand and a brush in the other, he stood on the ladder with his body leaning across the partition between two shower stalls. There he took his much-needed rest, emitting contented snores.

While visiting our closest town, Kabinburi, Gunilla experienced a situation where sleep really caught a Thai person unawares. Gunilla's car was stopped at a traffic light. When the light turned green, the car in front did not budge. The light switched back to red and still no movement. After the light turned green again, the other cars in the queue beeped their horns. The driver in the front car twitched and woke up from his lunch nap.

More alarming is that, in the countryside, one often sees vehicles that, for no obvious reason, have driven into a ditch. Probably a consequence of tropical slumber—or other reasons, as we shall see later.

6. Relations Between The Sexes

Less than a generation ago, it was legal and widely accepted for a Thai man to have more than one wife. It was even considered a status symbol for a wealthy man to have many wives. But for those who grew up in such an environment, the situation could be rough. Even today, men still

keep extra wives or mistresses, even though such relationships are not officially regarded as marriage. An extra wife is known as a *mia noi* or 'minor wife.' The wives live separately while the husband commutes between his 'families.' The woman commonly preserves the continuity in the family, while the husband plays more of a secondary role.

Thai women are often very independent. In the old agricultural society, they took care of both the house and farm while the husband was galavanting about. In modern Thai society, for many rural folk,

the traditional agricultural community has been replaced by life in the big city. Whole families are leaving their villages to be assimilated into modern industrial society. Or father will set out alone to find work.

A tourist in Bangkok will meet with obtrusive offers for sexual services, and may get the impression that the Thai people are sexually loose. Once, I was accosted by an energetic tout who enthusiastically showed me an accordion-card index of pretty girls. When I refused, he turned his image archive over to a collection of young boys.

Prostitution is big in Thailand and it has grown along with the tourism industry and the general economic upswing. But prostitution is nothing new in Thailand. The vast majority of sex establishments in this country—in one guise or another—cater to local customers, not foreigners. Recruiters for Thai brothels scour the countryside and offer parents money for their daughters who, in turn, will send them more money to repay them for the sacrifices of raising her. Then there are the well-documented bars that cater to foreigners. Both the girls from these establishments (and the parents) might get plenty of money from foreign customers, thus enabling them to take part in the consumer-orientated society, but traditional social patterns are being broken, often creating mental distress.

Elsewhere in traditional Thai society, the general attitude is what a Western foreigner would call conservative or even prudish. At the beach, very few Thai women wear swimsuits or the even more radical bikini. A 'respectable' woman swims in shorts and a T-shirt. Along the riverbanks in the rural areas, women wrap themselves in a sarong while taking a bath. Thai boys and girls commonly do not touch each other or make overt displays of affection toward one another in public, and even some married couples don't hold hands. This traditional attitude is, of course, more prevalent in the countryside. In the cities, nowadays, young people behave more or less as they please—although you will never see Thais openly kissing each other, as people do in Western societies.

It wasn't that long ago in the rural areas that a boy could be fined for touching a girl. It is, however, commonly accepted to demonstrate your friendship with a person of the same sex and, for instance, to hold hands with that person when out and about. Girls gladly put their arms around their girl friends, or hold hands with them (and boys do the same with their pals)—and it has no sexual connotation whatsoever. I once saw two generals on TV who walked holding hands during an inspection of a military unit on parade.

One incident in our company almost ended in catastrophe. Our little secretary Miau ('Cat') had resigned to continue her studies in Bangkok.

Our department head, Erik, made a farewell speech and presented her with a gift. The girl was moved to tears. Erik felt compelled to console her in the Swedish manner by giving her a big fatherly hug. But this had the opposite effect. Completely embarrassed, the girl broke down into uncontrollable sobs. Erik stood there crestfallen. He had unwittingly committed one of the worst social faux pas' imaginable in Thai society.

In the booming suburban areas around the industrial estates, a new way of life is emerging. Thousands of young people live together in congested living quarters. Thus the old social rules, maintained in the village, where several generations lived together in the same house, no longer have the same power.

Young people and couples are often forced to migrate from their home villages—but creating a new home in Thailand is not as complicated as in Western societies. In a nearby village I saw a boy and girl stop in front of a furniture and hardware shop. They walked around looking at household items, and it seemed as if they were about to move into a new apartment because they took a long time to decide on a mattress. The girl finally chose one with a teddy-bear pattern, and the boy chose a pink fan on a pedestal. When the girl started to look at plastic bowls and utensils, the boy became uninterested. He just shrugged his shoulders when she held up two types of bowl. They eventually paid for their stuff and the boy kick-started his motorbike. The girl jumped on the pillion holding the mattress in front of her and the fan and other goods under her arm. Then they rode off together. It doesn't have to be any more complicated than that in Thailand.

But young couples are in an awkward situation when expecting children. There are hardly any day-care facilities, and mothers are not prepared to, or are not able to, give up their working life. So the grandmother in the home village often has to bring up the grandchild. In rural Thai society today, many children grow up with their grandparents and only sporadically do they see their mum and dad.

But by sending their children to the grandparents, parents have at least provided a safe haven and an ordered existence—which simply cannot be found in the industrial areas where they live. Some Thai mothers leave the working life to take care of their children, but neither the cities nor the industrial areas are good places to bring up a child. So the mother takes the child and returns to her home village to live with her parents while the husband stays in the city to provide for his family.

Starting up a family creates a safety net for oneself and the children. Public institutions do not look after citizens, and one has to take responsibility for one's own relatives. Family unity in Thailand is built on both economic conditions and emotional bonds. In the absence of government social services, Thai family members need to support and take care of each other. Parents will moonlight to send their children to good schools, and if someone is sick, a relative provides care at the hospital or covers for the sick person at the workplace.

Work distribution between the sexes in Thailand can appear strange to a foreigner. In the countryside, women often do the heavy work while men operate the machines. When a rice paddy is to be ploughed, men operate the rotary cultivator ('mechanical buffalo') while women bend their backs to re-plant rice shoots.

When husband and wife ride a motorbike, it is always the man who drives. One day, at the petrol station, I got a wonderful demonstration of the Thai division of labour. A motorbike pulled up for a refill and the woman on the pillion put down the sack of rice she had under one arm.

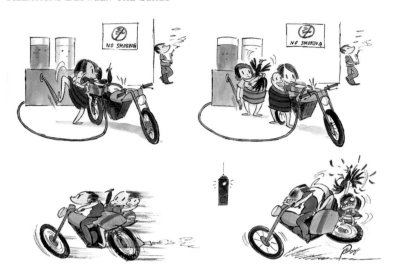

The man parked the bike and stood beside the pump to smoke a cigarette!—at which point I moved further away from the scene. A woman with a child on her hip approached to pump the petrol. She couldn't manage the pump handle one-handed, so the female passenger had to assist. She too, only had one hand to spare because she was gripping, under the other arm, the family's splendid rooster. Nevertheless, the two single-handed women managed to fill the tank while the man unhurriedly finished his smoke. He straddled the bike anew and the woman grabbed the rice sack. With the sack on her knee and the rooster under her arm, she departed with her husband, who got a no-doubt well-deserved break during the pit stop.

Many foreign men who come to Thailand are mezmerised by the pretty Thai women they meet at work or in more relaxed environments. Quite often a relationship develops, which may last for longer or shorter periods, but in many cases the ability to communicate with each other is limited—although this does not seem to create any obstacles for many foreigners, who fall in love well above their head. The Thai woman often has a totally different view on a lasting relationship with a man, and sees marriage to a large extent as a practical arrangement for economic security for her and her children. When a foreigner comes her way, it can be an excellent opportunity, considering that most are much better off financially than any Thai man she may catch. Older bachelors or newly divorced men are attractive prey for young Thai women looking for security.

In spite of the different cultural backgrounds and expectations, there are numerous examples of mixed marriages where the relationship has developed to mutual satisfaction. The foreigner has his pretty wife, who cares for him, and she has got a husband who can support her and her family economically. But there are also examples where the Thai girl has taken advantage of the situation in the most cruel way. During my years working in Thailand, I have seen many relationships develop and crash.

Some time ago, a number of experts from Europe were invited to assist with improving production efficiency in the mill. A couple of very experienced papermakers arrived on site and were confronted with all types of difficulties. They worked hard and their wives, who were still in Europe, were told to wait until their husbands had better control of the situation before joining them in Thailand. The monsoon season was still very evident, with heavy rainfall almost every day, so there was no recommendation that the wives come to Thailand for some time.

In the evenings the foreigners explored the local entertainment venues and soon became acquainted with the young women often found at such places. The overweight Ralf soon took a liking to one of the girls. They met regularly in the evenings and, before long, the girl moved into his house. It was obvious that they enjoyed each other's company, even though there were communication difficulties to start with.

Ralf's wife in Europe gradually became more and more anxious to come to Thailand, but Ralf insisted that he still had too much work to do and the rain was still pouring down every day. Soon, Ralf's wife got suspicious, and one day she called Ralf and announced that she had bought air tickets and would arrive the next Friday evening. The Thai girl, Nit, had to find a temporary place to stay, and she moved to a friend down the street, just before Ralf's wife, Anne, arrived.

Anne was a practical woman who immediately started to clean the house, as her husband had neglected his domestic duties in her absence. She found a closed wardrobe and asked Ralf for the key. He had, of course, never seen any key for this wardrobe, and he had never opened it. The following day, after Ralf had left for the factory, Anne managed, with the skills of a suspicious woman, to open the wardrobe doors—and there she found Nit's outfits all lined up and neatly folded away. When Ralf returned in the evening, he was confronted by a wife with many questions. Not long afterwards, Anne decided to pack her belongings and return to Europe.

Anne's taxi had just turned the corner when Nit appeared from the far end of the street. There could be no time allowed for Ralf to think the matter over, and she had to move fast. She had made good progress and could not let him off the hook now. With her most sacred possession, a big picture of the highly revered King Chulalongkorn, under her arm, she walked back to Ralf's house, and soon life was back to normal again. After completing his contract with the company, Ralf returned to Europe with Nit, and now lives a happy family life with her and their pretty little daughter.

Not all stories have a happy end like this. At the Bangkok university where I occasionally lecture, I came across a sad story. A middle-aged German bachelor with a solid academic background was invited to take

a position as assistant professor. He had lived all his life with his mother in Germany, and moving to Bangkok was a big upheaval for him. He was well taken care of, and the faculty staff did everything to help him settle into this new and strange environment. A young female faculty member and her boyfriend introduced him to the social life in Bangkok, and soon they became friends.

One day the young woman, Lek, looked very distressed, and Wolfgang enquired cautiously about her problem. Well, her boyfriend had broken their relationship and she was totally lost. Wolfgang tried to comfort Lek, and his concealed feelings gradually came to the surface.

After a short period of intense courtship, Wolfgang mustered all his courage and proposed to Lek. It was a very merry wedding party, and everyone expected a long and successful marriage. The newly wedded couple needed an appropriate home, and they soon found a nice house. It is, of course, less complicated to have a Thai person registered as the formal house owner, and when they bought the new car to go with it, there was no hesitation on Wolfgang's part at having the car also registered in Lek's name.

It is difficult to say what they had expected from their marriage besides the passion and the need for mutual comfort, but after some time Lek did not feel comfortable with Wolfgang and she requested a divorce. Wolfgang, who was a very considerate person, accepted that the different personal and cultural backgrounds made living together difficult, and he

accepted. Now the hard facts became evident to Wolfgang. The house and the car belonged to Lek, and he had to give up everything he had invested in their common future. It was a very distressed Wolfgang who returned to his bachelor life, and his despair was far from relieved when he later found out that Lek's former boyfriend had moved in with her in the house and was using the car Wolfgang had bought.

7. Time Without Limits

In the West, we equate time with money—and construct formulas that show how much money we can make or lose per unit of time. Our time is limited and we have to achieve as much as possible within a fixed period, whether that means a business trip to Thailand, the company's financial year, or our own life span. Our lives have a finite limit, and we only have one, so we really have to make the most of it. Eventually, on Judgement Day, we have to account for our deeds. This view of existence makes the Westerner very vulnerable in Thai society.

Eastern philosophies look upon the concept of time in a totally different way. Time is eternal and has neither beginning nor end. The concept of an 'eon' is sometimes used to state an almost infinite length of time. A Chinese philosopher described an eon as follows: imagine the largest mountain on earth, and then take a thread of silk and stroke the mountain's top. When you have finally worn down the mountain to a plain, only a fraction of an eon will have passed. So why be in such a hurry when what needs to be done will probably get done eventually anyway?

In the West, we draw our life span as a straight line starting at birth, with milestones like marriage and child birth along the way, and a rather predictable ending. In the East, life is looked upon as a circle, and when one revolution in a life cycle is completed, one is reborn in a new form. Therefore, there is no compulsion to complete a certain task at a certain time due to some agreed plan.

What happens when a Western businessman comes to Bangkok on a three-day visit to settle a deal? He brings a proposal for an agreement in his briefcase and doesn't see any reason why his Thai counterpart cannot sign the contract. But it is almost inevitable that their negotiations will take a different turn. The Thai—after a long period of small talk, socializing, and general procrastination—will want to make changes to the contract

and add a number of more or less complicated clauses to cover the most unlikely eventualities.

Time passes while the negotiations drag on and the Thai makes new demands for long-term credit and extensive guarantees, and inserts new clauses regarding damage claims. The set time for the trip draws to a close and there is still no signed contract in sight. At this point the Westerner has to make a final decision. Should he return home empty-handed, or accept what might be an unfavourable deal?

The Thai has all the time in the world on his side and doesn't mind the foreigner going home for consultations; instead, he exploits the situation to the breaking point. The foreigner has lost any upper hand he might have had, and the Thai simply sits and waits for his demands to be met. It is the foreigner who has to take the next step and put forward a compromise that doesn't differ too much from the Thai's proposal.

The Westerner who comes to work in Thailand usually ends up experiencing the sapping of time. He may be on a short-term contract and is expected to finish his assignment within two or three years. Initially this seems fairly long—certainly time enough—and allows room for some tropical delays. But fixed schedules do not have the same status in Thailand that we assign them in the West. When a project's milestones haven't been reached, the Thais simply declare, without any qualms, that they didn't finish on time, but the job will most likely be finished soon.

To make up for the delay, Westerners will draw up an action plan and make sure that everybody involved is aware of the importance of finishing the project on time. Everyone shakes hands and the Western manager breathes a sigh of relief at getting the project back on track again. Unfortunately, he'll likely be just as disappointed at the next follow-up, when he realizes that, in spite of all the handshaking, progress has been very modest. The Thai attitude is: why does all this have to be done during this stressed-out foreigner's time in Thailand? Can't he stay a few more years or send a new project manager to enjoy life here? But the Westerner will view his time in Thailand as a personal and professional failure if he hasn't met the goals assigned to him by his company.

The Thais' relaxed attitude makes it hard for them to be on time. It is almost exceptional if a Thai shows up at an agreed time and place. And, to a Western way of thinking, they use the most improbable excuses. In

Bangkok, people usually blame the traffic. But to some Westerners this is still unacceptable. After all, Thais who have lived all their lives in Bangkok should be able to judge the amount of time needed to cross the city. Shouldn't they? Other reasons for late arrival are that they had a lot to do, that they wanted to finish what they were doing, or simply had other things to do. For Thais it is also fully acceptable to say that you have been out to eat. These excuses are valid, even to senior managers, and it isn't unheard of to let your managing director sit and wait for half an hour. The director can in turn let the whole management team sit and wait in the conference room for an hour while he attends to some other task. A Westerner considers this behaviour as showing extreme disrespect for other people's time, but if you view time as endless, as the Thais do, then keeping other people waiting for a while is not such a big deal.

You discover another aspect of the Thai concept of infinite time when you try to make up a work schedule. Thais in authority usually acquire a big, leather-bound diary that they carry around as a symbol of their standing. But having a diary doesn't necessarily imply that they actually use it as a planning tool. This extends to even a simple task such as agreeing to a time for a meeting with a superior. You do this through a secretary, who makes a brave attempt to keep track of her boss's comings and goings. But the secretary can't give a firm answer because the boss might be busy at the anticipated time or hasn't decided what he will be doing—so she can't give you an appointment. She has to consult with her boss before answering. If you eventually do manage to schedule a meeting, you still can't be certain that it will happen at the arranged time. Maybe the Thai will suddenly make other plans that will reverse all prior engagements.

A Thai's planning is usually very short-term, and he does what is judged appropriate for the moment. I wonder how much this attitude has to do with Thai history and climate. In some places in the West, we have always had to plan at least one year ahead to survive winter. One had to stockpile food, fuel, and warm clothes. In Thailand, people have never had to worry about such things, except perhaps for the storing of rainwater ahead of the long, hot, dry months. And even then, there was little work to do in such preparation, as it either rained or it didn't, and your jars became full or not as a result.

A Thai has difficulties in imagining problems that don't make themselves instantly obvious. For instance, we wanted our landlord to check our roof during the dry season, in anticipation of the coming monsoon. It wasn't until the rainy season, when we were frantically putting out buckets to catch dripping water, that we received any response from the landlord.

Our production managers met with the same attitude when they wanted to introduce planned preventative maintenance shutdowns in the factory. Wasn't that completely unnecessary and a total waste of time, since the factory was doing so well? Why stop the machines at that stage? One year later, when breakdowns on the production line skyrocketed, management wanted to know why.

8. Body Language

The body has its own language in Thailand and a foreigner can often make unforgivable mistakes. The head is the noblest part of the body, and you should never touch or pat a Thai on the head. The feet are considered the lowest, and you should never display your soles or point them toward anyone. The Western habit of putting one's feet up on the desk is unspeakably impolite. Energetically waving your arms to call a taxi shows you lack a proper upbringing. (Stretch your arm out at waist level and use a gentle flagging motion with your hand.)

Thai society is extremely hierarchical. The Thai gesture of greeting, the *wai*, is a demonstration of respect for another person. The higher you hold your fingertips in front of you, the higher the respect for the person you greet. Parents teach their children from an early age to *wai* correctly, and the rules are engraved in their minds. Children *wai* their parents, servants *wai* guests, and subordinates *wai* their boss. It is always the person with the lower status who *wais* first; the one of higher status who responds, putting his fingertips on a lower level than the subordinate. It is not always necessary to return the greeting: normally you do not *wai* servants and children. A Buddhist monk never returns the respectful *wai* from the faithful Thais.

When Robert and his wife returned from their first weekend visit to Bangkok, Robert told me they had literally been thrown out of the sacred temple, Wat Phra Keo. He described how they had been standing in a line and were inspecting the murals. They then came upon the famed Emerald Buddha on a high, gold-plated pedestal. Robert leaned toward his wife and put his arm around her shoulders to point out an object near the Buddha figure. You may not have spotted them, but here were three serious breaches of etiquette that became too much for the temple guards. You should never stand up in front of a Buddha figure; you are

not, at least not in a temple, allowed to embrace another person, even your spouse; and you should never point a finger at the Buddha.

Thai people squat on their haunches whenever and wherever. In the market-place, vendors squat amongst their goods with their elbows resting on their knees. In doorways, shopkeepers sit comfortably slouched, looking like nestling chicks. In the countryside, people squat at bus stops, waiting for transport. I don't know whether this is because of long training from early childhood, or because of a unique anatomical finesse that the Thais (and most other Asians) are graced with, but I suspect the latter. Given this, it can sometimes lead to amusing moments when Thais have to adjust to a work environment created by foreigners.

One of our Western managers equipped his repair shop with workbenches of ergonomically correct height. So he was disappointed when he found his mechanics squatting on their heels on the floor to change the bearing of a pump. He urged them to use the workbenches to work more comfortably. When he returned later, he saw that they had moved the pump up onto the bench and were now comfortably squatting beside it on the work surface, continuing their repairs.

I too, had set up a QC laboratory with workbenches along the walls, and sets of drawers and cupboards under the benches. I had left space

clear underneath the benches so that the workers would have enough leg-room. In my drawings for the installation, I had marked these areas with "space for sitting work," but this information was completely misunderstood. Instead, they crept in underneath the benches and used these small compartments as cosy writing places. Obviously the average foreigner would never have come up with this novel use, because he couldn't possibly have fitted into these tiny retreats.

I always felt a bit embarrassed when the office maid entered my office to deliver the daily post. She always approached my desk with a crouching walk and lowered her head to show respect. I probably made work awkward for my Thai co-workers by ignoring my superior position. In the Swedish way, I preferred walking around to guide my staff while they were sitting at their workplaces. I sometimes sat down on my heels beside them to explain or help with a certain task, but they would immediately rush off and get a chair for me. It was totally out of the question for a boss to sit beside a worker with his head lower than his subordinate.

Chairs aren't always found in homes in the countryside. Instead, people sit on the floor. Even in urban Thai society, the habit of sitting with crossed legs on the floor is still deeply rooted. Our office girls prefer to sit on chairs with their legs crossed underneath them and their pillow behind their backs. I tried to do this too, but fell over with the chair on top of me.

One New Year's Eve, my staff arranged a street party and invited me and some other foreigners along. As usual, everyone joined in the preparation for a huge number of dishes. I was entrusted with cutting the vegetables for the salad. Eventually it was time to put out all the food bowls. I looked around for the tables and chairs but it was, of course, a street party, so we spread mats out and sat down in a big circle around a sea of bowls. I folded my legs underneath me and sat down to eat. After a while, my legs fell asleep and, with a certain effort, I managed to hoist myself up into a standing position. Small smiles were exchanged among the staff, who found their seats on the ground perfectly comfortable. The food remained where it was, of course, so I had to lower myself back down to the ground.

Even if the Thais display a flexibility that would make a Russian gymnast envious, they can, at the same time, seem very inactive. I greatly impressed the locals by going for a jog in the evenings. Gunilla arranged, along with some other foreign wives, a workout programme to stay in shape. They invited some Thai ladies to join them—and there were many excuses why they could not. The girl next door replied to the invitation with something akin to horror in her voice. She told us that she had a cousin who once tried to do aerobics. The cousin had gotten aches all over her body after the first workout and immediately ceased such "dangerous" exercise.

Most Thais are very conscious of their surroundings, and they dress accordingly. Thailand's climate is hot all year round, but that doesn't mean you can expose your body for public view.

In the business world, a formal dress code prevails, with long-sleeved shirts and trousers for men. The Western-style neck-tie is gradually gaining acceptance among those who want to demonstrate the importance of their position. Women often wear a jacket and skirt ensemble with stockings. In government offices, clerks wear military style uniforms with scores of badges, medals, and ribbons for who knows what.

In school, children are usually dressed in uniforms consisting of white blouses and dark-blue skirts for the girls, and white shirts and khaki shorts for the boys. In the morning, when the children assemble in front of the flagpole for the national anthem, the teachers inspect them to make sure that they are dressed correctly, just like an army sergeant major would do with a platoon of soldiers. In the countryside, especially, where incomes are considerably less than in the towns and cities, it's amazing how mothers and grandmothers manage to make their children look so spick and span for school every day. Unfortunately, for the fashion conscious, the uniform is compulsory and there is no possibility to impress ones friends by wearing fancy clothes to class. The female teachers, if not dressed in official uniform, often wear colourful dresses, whereas male teachers are more conservatively dressed.

A remarkable transformation takes place amongst the older teenage girls in our village when they are not at college or university. In the evenings they dress in colourful T-shirts and shorts, to sing karaoke songs and hang out with their friends. But in the mornings they line up along the roadside waiting for buses or pick-up trucks, neat and tidy in their formal black skirts and white blouses, looking like sophisticated young ladies.

There is poor understanding amongst Thais of the Western tendency to wear little clothing because of the hot climate. When confronted with such a spectacle, Thais look on incredulously—and with some degree of amusement and a great deal of embarrassment. The tourist on the beach wearing only swimwear in the blazing sun is considered next to insane—but his behaviour is tolerated as long as he stays on the beach. For Western women, going topless on the popular tourist beaches is also tolerated—although not really approved of. But, as mentioned previously, don't ever expect to see Thai ladies on the beach in anything other than shorts and T-shirt—even when swimming. When tourists appear in the city still wearing beachwear, most Thais frown and think it very bad manners. Dress like this in the city and you'll be the subject of countless sniggers, but most Thais will simply look away in embarrassment.

Many Thais consider scanty female clothing—like short skirts without stockings, or tops with bare shoulders—as the standard attire for bargirls, and they are confused when they meet Western women dressed in a similar way. The industrial park where our mill is located is home to a large number of international companies. Many of these firms

have foreigners from the parent company working together with Thai employees. In most cases these foreigners hold senior positions—and the Thai staff always pays a certain respect to their superiors. Now and then, European women appear at the industrial park on short-term contracts. During a pleasant summer in Europe, a very relaxed attitude prevails, but coming to Thailand with the same habits can certainly create confusion. The modern European dress code is much more flexible than in Thailand, if the following example is anything to go by: A young European woman on assignment to one of the companies in our industrial park found the weather uncomfortably hot, and she thought that less formal attire would make the working day more bearable. When she arrived in the office one morning dressed in mini-shorts and a top with bare shoulders, her Thai male colleagues didn't know where to look. This was the type of outfit worn by the girls serving their beer the previous evening. The girls in the office simply looked at each other and smiled at the Western woman in a disrespectful way.

9. Dangers

Friends and relatives told us all about the dangers that were waiting for us in Thailand, so we were well prepared for snakes, tigers, and tropical diseases. The Thai mosquito didn't impress us much at first, but, in spite of its small size, it is a savage rascal that soon took a liking to Gunilla. It rejected me from the outset, being, as most Thais are, a gourmet. The mosquitoes in Thailand are not very loud. They sneak into our bedroom in the tropical night and attack Gunilla while I sleep totally unconcerned beside her. Like the Thais, they are not voracious eaters, preferring to nibble continuously on the tastiest bits—and leaving a bunch of irritating, red calling cards behind. Nordic mosquitoes approach more honestly with their annoying buzz in the summer night, so that you have to pull your blanket over your head to get any sleep.

In the beginning, Gunilla was bitten all over, and even accused the mosquitoes of crawling underneath the blankets to bite her in the most sensitive places. We soon bought a mosquito net and solved that problem

Malaria-carrying mosquitoes are present in Thailand, but in most of the country there is little danger. The horrible dengue fever, spread by a different kind of mosquito, is a more common threat. Gunilla deployed a formidable arsenal of mosquito sticks and sprays to keep the pests at bay. It was hard to appreciate the smell of her perfume over the cloying mosquito spray when we went out for dinner in the evenings.

Gunilla also wages a war of attrition in our house against other little invaders. Ants search out tiny food scraps and invite their whole family for a party. If we forget to wipe the kitchen table properly at night, or drop a single rice grain, we are greeted in the morning with a dark ribbon of ants marching under the door, up the wall, and over the table. Gunilla

sets up poison traps, but the ants soon find ways to get in. Their most innovative approach to the kitchen table has been through the electric socket in the wall above, from where they invade in hordes. A good spray of insecticide keeps them at bay for a couple of days.

Our stand-alone food cupboard sits on high legs positioned in special trays (filled daily with water) that stop the ants from climbing up the legs. It is important not to leave anything on top of the cupboard that touches the wall and creates a bridge for the ants. I did this once with a loaf of bread. A day later, nothing was left except a fine powder and a retreating army of bloated ants.

One of Gunilla's morning rituals is to make a small drum-roll with her toothbrush against the sink, to get rid of any drowsy ants who slept among the bristles after partying the night before.

We eventually got used to having small domestic guests. We just had to accept the small lizards scurrying all over the walls. After all, they do some good by catching the odd mosquito.

There are, of course, animals that you should look out for. A neighbour left his shoes outside the house, as is customary, during his lunch break. When he put them back on, he received a painful sting. An exhausted scorpion had taken refuge in one of the shoes for its own lunchtime siesta. Every now and then, a snake will visit our house. Even if they aren't of the most venomous variety, we Swedes have a healthy respect for snakes. We don't just walk up and take the snake by its neck and toss it away like the Thais do.

But even the snakes find it too warm at times, and are drawn to the air-conditioned flow that finds its way out of our house. Sometimes an undulating serpent's head will appear outside our glass front door looking to find a way in to the cool. In the kitchen we often leave the door open to air out excess chilli fumes. We have a screen door to keep creatures out, but one day a snake was banging vigorously at it, driven frantic by the cooking smells coming from the pot. Gunilla tried to drive him off with a broomstick, but a Thai snake doesn't let himself be distracted that easily from a tempting chilli stew. Not until Gunilla ran to get her camera did the snake disappear into a drain, obviously camera-shy.

Stray dogs are abundant in Thailand, but don't usually constitute a threat—though it does sometimes feel uncomfortable to have so many unsupervised canines around. Packs of dogs that live close to eating houses or vendors' carts make short work of all food scraps. With plenty of places to eat, there are plenty of dogs—most in depressingly bad condition. In Thailand (except in the province of Sakhon Nakhon), people usually don't eat dog, as is the custom in some parts of Laos and Vietnam—where you are not troubled by many stray dogs roaming the streets. The Thais, on the contrary, usually care for all their stray mongrels and look upon the dog eaters with a certain contempt. In most cases you don't have to worry about Thai street dogs; they are just waiting to snatch up some food. In between meals they just lie around, so motionless you wonder if they are still alive. But it is hot for dogs, too, and a shady spot in the street is as good a place as any for sleeping.

But the biggest dangers in Thailand do not come from the animal kingdom. Traffic accidents claim a huge number of victims—not surprising considering the generally abysmal driving habits. Traffic accidents are also a main cause of foreign visitors being sent home prematurely. Motorcyclists are the most endangered road species in any country, but considering the lack of protective gear in Thailand, it doesn't take a big fall for a bike rider to get quite messed up.

The most serious accidents involve heavy trucks. Traffic is intense on the bigger country roads. The trucks are sometimes driven 24 hours a day by the same driver. So it is not unusual for him to fall asleep at the wheel. Not surprisingly, one popular drink sold at petrol stations and convenience stores is a caffeine stimulant tincture sold in small brown bottles. These bottles may be found in drifts in roadside ditches—next to the overturned trucks.

If, in spite of all precautions, you fall victim to wild animals or a traffic accident, there is help at hand, even upcountry. One evening, I was bitten on the calf by a dog while out on my regular jog. The company's ambulance took me to the local hospital, a good ten kilometres away, where I was treated with antibiotics and given tetanus and rabies vaccinations. This hospital didn't look impressive at all, but the medical attendants worked efficiently and, even though I made a number return visits for the rabies jabs and to check on the wound, I never had to wait for more than a couple of minutes. The staff were skilled in taking care of minor injuries from motorbike falls, dog bites, and a myriad of other upcountry hazards.

It takes a good level of care to prevent infections in this warm and humid climate, but once in a while, I did raise my eyebrows at practices that would be unthinkable in a Swedish clinic. The hospital's motorbike, emblazoned with the Red Cross, stood in the open-air waiting area. During one of my visits, a nurse had to make a house call. An assistant kick-started the bike, the nurse jumped on behind with her medical bag, and they puttered off between the waiting-room benches.

At the reception counter one morning, a young man was standing in front of me with a large and magnificent rooster under one arm. The bird looked a bit peaky and his head drooped as limp as spaghetti, so I asked the man, jokingly, if the rooster was ill. The man laughed and said that the bird wasn't feeling too well. He himself had difficulties filling out the registration form, since he only had one hand free, so I helped him keep the paper still. In the meantime, the rooster rested his head on top of the desk, looking decidedly unwell. But I never really found out if the man was at the hospital for himself or the bird.

Patients at the local hospital are taken care of efficiently in a steady stream. In the emergency room, four cots with plastic coating are lined up along one wall. In between patients, the nurses wipe the cots down with a cloth. When a lad who had taken a fall from his motorbike came in after the rooster, his mates gathered around him to laugh as he yelled in protest when the nurse poured disinfectant on his cuts. Nearby was a small desk where another nurse tried her best to keep track of medical records with all the ruckus going on around her.

One morning, when I went to the hospital to check up on my bite wound, that small desk had been completely taken over by a big bowl of rice and many smaller bowls filled with spicy dishes. Seated around the

desk, the nurses helped themselves to the food while the patients on the cots had to wait a while to be seen to. In Thailand, never get in the way of anyone and their lunch—even if you're walking wounded!

The Swedish health authorities might object to some public health care practices in the Thai countryside, but I experienced a very relaxed atmosphere during my visits, and received personal attention the likes of which I never found in Sweden.

It's a very different picture in the big private hospitals of Bangkok. In the reception halls of these places, you get the feeling of entering a five-star hotel: wall-to-wall carpeting; sofas with decoratively arranged pillows; and a hostess who greets you, inquiring what kind of problem you have, and how she can be of assistance.

One Saturday evening, during a dinner with friends in Bangkok, I was stricken with sharp pains in the abdomen and rushed to a nearby private hospital. I didn't have to wait long before a doctor had diagnosed a gallstone. Fifteen minutes later, I lay with a drip in a private room that looked like a hotel suite, awaiting further developments. I was put through a series of examinations, and by noon on Sunday I was on the operating table undergoing a peephole operation that left only tiny cuts on my stomach. I had to endure two whole days in that terrible sickroom — furnished only with sofa and armchairs, a well-stocked pantry, and a TV and video—before the doctor would let me get back to the countryside.

Of course, this kind of health care isn't free and you have make sure that you have private insurance.

But sometimes the advanced medical care available in Bangkok may require assistance from traditional practices. During a mountain hike in Bhutan in the Himalayas, Gunilla slipped on a steep footpath and had a bad fall. She felt a terrible pain in her ankle and our guides had to carry her down the last kilometre to a waiting car. At the hospital in Thimpu, the X-ray revealed three bone fractures, and a temporary cast was made, as we were flying back to Bangkok the following day.

At the hospital in Bangkok, the orthopaedic surgeon didn't see any other alternative than surgery to mend the breaks. The operation was performed later the same day and left eight screws in Gunilla's ankle. She left the hospital a few days later on crutches, with strict orders to rest the leg for a couple of months.

With no heavy old-fashioned cast, the injury didn't look very serious to our neighbours in the village, and they couldn't understand why Gunilla could not start walking again. They suggested that she consult a local 'spirit doctor' who had helped many people in the surrounding villages with similar injuries such as gun-shot wounds and bone fractures. Most of his patients had apparently made very quick recoveries, and the man had a good reputation for his healing skills.

Preparations had to be made for the arrival of the *mor phaenboraan*, the spirit doctor. Rice grains were spread on a plate and an egg placed on top; yellow candles were set in banana-leaf cones and positioned beside the egg; then a bottle of local liquor was placed next to the plate. When the old doctor arrived in the evening, he spread a handkerchief on the floor in front of the plate and lit a candle. With the candle held between his palms, he raised his hands in a *wai* in front of his face, closed his eyes, and, in a low voice, called upon the spirit world to assist in his healing mission. When his exhortations were complete, he pulled out a small brown bottle from his pocket and unscrewed the cap. He brought the bottle and the candle close to Gunilla's ankle and blew over the flame and the mouth of the bottle. He then poured some oily, fragrant liquid from the bottle into his hands and rubbed it on Gunilla's ankle—at which she reported a strange sensation spreading along her leg. Finally he brought his hands together in another *wai* and raised his eyes skyward in thanks to the spirits for their assistance.

Over the next few weeks, the *mor phaenboraan* returned to our home and repeated his ceremony a number of times. It is difficult to say to what extent the spirits contributed to Gunilla's recovery—and we'll never know what would have happened without them—but by respecting the local traditions, our neighbours felt they had made a good contribution to her well-being. In any case, it brought some extra comfort and at least provided an entertaining placebo effect during her confinement to crutches.

10. With Buddha As A Passenger

When we stepped out of the airport terminal for the first time, it was not only the humid tropical air that hit us, but also the deafening traffic noise. A double-decker motorway runs next to the airport, winding its way into the centre of Bangkok. Our driver unconcernedly steered the car out into the intense traffic and, with our hearts in our mouths, we saw that he was driving on the wrong side of the road. Well, it wasn't that bad of course—traffic moves on the left in Thailand—but, we later learned, people are flexible in this regard as well as with other regulations.

The motorway was packed with cars. Lanes, as such, didn't exist. As soon as a gap appeared somewhere, our driver managed to sneak in with an incredible weaving technique. Even though the traffic appeared totally

undisciplined, the mass of cars still flowed slowly forwards. No doubt, the Thais' ability to control their emotions helps here. In our car there was a little Buddha sitting on the dashboard with a wreath of flowers around him, looking out of the windscreen at the traffic. We later heard that the strange squiggles in white and gold paint, daubed on the ceiling of the car, indicated that it had been blessed by a Buddhist monk. With a blessed car and a Buddha statuette sitting on the dash, why would a driver have to worry about traffic dangers?

Western safety norms are not valid in Thailand. Instead, one comes across every conceivable, and inconceivable, way of driving and riding in a vehicle. In the countryside, the most common vehicles are pick-up trucks and little motorbikes that buzz around like bees let loose from the hive. These trucks and motorbikes have an incredible transport capacity, even given the small stature of Thais. As many people as possible squeeze together in a truck, and then a few more cram themselves on board. Men sit in a row on the edge of the pick-up bed and don't seem to have any problem staying onboard. Women and children sit crammed together in the middle. If the bed isn't big enough, the problem is easily solved by building an extra floor and stowing the passengers on two layers. Or putting up a few hammocks to cater for the sleeping option. A few people on top of the driver's cab give counter-weight to the load in the bed, and so prevent the front wheels from lifting off the road.

Thailand is awash with small motorbikes. Pretty soon we fell for the temptation ourselves, and acquired a small Suzuki runabout for local transport. The most common size comes with a 110-cc, two-stroke engine. The dealer warmed up to this particular model and enthusiastically explained that four people could ride on it in comfort. But we thought that two would be quite enough. Almost everyone has a motorbike like this. As soon as they can reach gear shift and foot-brakes, children happily ride to school with younger siblings as passengers. Too many brothers and sisters means the smallest clings to the back of a big sister.

The Thais ride their motorbikes as if it were the most natural thing in the world. If it starts raining, they simply hold up an umbrella with one hand and continue to steer single-handedly. Office girls in their neat dress suits sit side-saddle on motorbike taxis and take the opportunity to do their make-up or polish their nails. They have no need to cling to the driver, even when rounding corners. Thais totally trust their natural balance, which is of a whole different calibre to that of most foreigners.

When the family is going into town, the father drives the bike. The smallest child sits up front, in between dad's legs, holding the handlebars. Mum sits behind. The middle child is squeezed in between mum and dad, or else stands on the saddle gripping dad's shoulders. The oldest child clings to mum's back. Mother may also have a small child on each knee. There are all kinds of variations, but with more than three children, it becomes difficult to bring everyone along. This might be one reason why population growth in Thailand is in decline nowadays. In the old days, the cart behind the water buffalo allowed for a bigger family!

The motorbike is not only used for passenger transport, but for all kinds of other needs. It's like a circus performance on the country roads, where people have perfected the art of driving a motorbike with one hand, since the other is often needed to keep a load in place. When a builder is on his way from a wood trader, he balances a bunch of boards on one shoulder and steers with the one free arm. When a farmer goes to a cock-fight, he grips his rooster firmly around the legs and the bird gets to enjoy the wind in its feathers. A dog stands on its hind legs between his master's legs, front paws on the handlebars; but a sow for market is tied to a plank on the back.

Because they start riding motorbikes as children, young Thais soon become expert riders and get a kick out of showing off. Once, on our way home from Bangkok, our car was overtaken by a young lad on a motorbike. He pulled ahead of us just in front of our car, enjoying the 100 kilometres per hour speed. He was wearing standard motorbike attire: T-shirt, shorts, and thongs. He then began his performance. He climbed up and stood on the saddle with his hands still on the handlebars, then lay down on his stomach with his feet pointing straight out. He weaved skillfully in front of us until, after a while, he thought we had seen enough and waved goodbye. With his thongs still pointing straight back, he accelerated and was gone over the horizon at full speed.

It is easy to assume that no traffic rules exist in Thailand, but they do. Everyone needs a licence to drive legally and—astonishingly—you are not allowed to have more than two persons on a motorbike, and they must wear helmets. But everything is flexible. Wearing a helmet in the heat is uncomfortable, and if one keeps to the neighbourhood, a driver's licence isn't really necessary, is it? The police pull vehicles over if they have been speeding or to check the licence. In most cases, a minor violation can be taken care of on the spot. The most common method is to tuck a bill of a suitable denomination under one's licence when the policeman asks to look at it. If the bill is of a sufficiently high value, the incident should end with no more than a caution to drive more carefully.

The system of paying 'fines' directly to the policeman without any receipt might be unfamiliar or unsavoury to foreigners, but it is really very practical, as it avoids a lot of the administrative hassle that makes collecting fines such a burden in Western society. Besides, the ordinary policeman in Thailand gets a very modest salary. He can barely survive himself, much less provide for his family, so he has to find alternative means of income. He might, for instance, get paid to stand and direct the traffic outside a big company office during rush hour, or to hang around in banks or jewellers' shops as a deterrent to armed robbers. There are many ways to make money by wearing a uniform, but the policeman doesn't get to keep all of the extra income. Some must to go to his boss, who naturally can't survive on his salary either. In this way an entire 'professional' police corps can be maintained without overly burdening the Treasury.

Many drivers do have a licence in Thailand, if for no other reason than to facilitate proceedings if an accident should occur. No insurance company pays any compensation if the driver doesn't hold a licence. There are driving schools in Thailand, but there are also easier ways to obtain a licence. A driver's licence is issued by the traffic authorities in each provincial capital. As a foreigner, I had to provide numerous documents before being entrusted with a Thai licence: certificates from the employer and from the district office to prove residence in Thailand;

a work permit; a residence permit; and a certificate of health. Across the street from the licence department was a clinic that provided this latter service. I was requested to fill in my name on the application form, which was then stamped, and I had to pay twenty baht. After waiting for a while, I found myself standing with the health certificate in hand.

"What about the medical check-up?"

"You have already received the certificate!"

I had to be grateful, and so I trotted off across the street for the next stop in getting a licence.

At the traffic office, I had to get all my documents examined and do a theoretical test. As a foreigner, I needed help to read the multiple-choice test. The questions were quite tricky. For instance:

A. How do you show that you want to turn right?

1) By holding out your right arm at a 90-degree angle.

2) By holding out your right arm at a 45-degree angle.

3) By waving your hand while holding your right arm at a 45-degree angle.

B. At what distance from the road junction do you have to indicate that you want to turn right?

1) 25 metres.

2) 35 metres.

3) 45 metres.

C. How far from the pavement should you park?

1) 10 cm.

2) 20 cm.

3) 30 cm.

The clerk sat with the answers in hand, helping me to put the ticks in the right boxes. The Thai aspirants are not treated as benevolently, but that problem can be taken care of smoothly. After filling in the test sheet, some people simply clip a 100-baht bill underneath it.

I then took my practical test in the car park outside. The clerk remained in his office, looking out through his window to make sure that I could drive the vehicle around the perimeter and then park it in the marked space. With the last hurdle over, the driver's licence was printed out while I waited; I paid eighty baht to the cashier and got a receipt. Finally I could step out on the road as a registered driver.

Luckily, those small Buddha figures sit on the dashboards of almost every vehicle, otherwise it is doubtful whether the traffic system would work at all in Thailand.

11. Water

Few things have had as large an impact on Thai society as water, which plays a fundamental role in the country's transportation, culture, and festivals. Thai culture has been built up around rice cultivation and fisheries. King Ramkamhaeng gathered the diverse Thai people under his banner in the first Siamese monarchy 700 years ago, leaving a famous stone inscription that his kingdom of Sukhothai was a good place to live, with rice in the fields and fish in the rivers.

The climate in Thailand is divided into two dry seasons—one much hotter than the other, both lasting around three months—and the rainy season, which lasts for almost half the year. In the transition between these seasons, the Thais celebrate the festivals of Songkran, in April, and Loy Kratong, in November. Both have water as their main theme.

Loy Kratong is celebrated at the full moon in November, when the rains have usually stopped for the year. People gather in the evening at a watercourse—the sea, rivers, streams, canals, lakes, and ponds—to launch their *kratongs*, little floats made out of banana leaves and decorated with flowers and candles. It is an incredibly beautiful experience to watch hundreds of these illuminated *kratongs* float away, along with their sponsors' troubles and woes, into the night. The festival was traditionally regarded as a sign of gratitude for the year's rain and a wish for a good rice crop. People also make a personal wish as they launch their *kratongs*.

Songkran is the traditional Thai New Year and the start of the agricultural year. It is a joyful celebration—held at the hottest time of year—in which water is poured over a Buddha statue to symbolically bathe him. After this ceremonial bathing, the festival degenerates into a

free-for-all water fight that lasts for the next three days. After this, rural Thais can confidently look forward to the coming monsoon that will drench the fields so that the rice cycle can start for another year.

Westerners from northern climes experience rain as unpleasant and cold, but rain in the tropics is warm and there is no danger in getting wet, as long as one doesn't enter air-conditioning afterwards. I had heard about the heavy rains in Thailand, and equipped myself with a full set of waterproof clothing from Sweden. One day, when the rain was pouring down, I got on my motorbike in my rain gear and caused quite a stir. Never before had the local people seen anything quite like it, and never before had I received so much general attention.

One Sunday afternoon during the rainy season, Gunilla and I were riding our motorbike to a restaurant. Suddenly the sky turned completely black and a few heavy raindrops began to burst on our heads. We just made it to a *sala*—an open-air shelter, like a gazebo, found along the country roads—before it came pouring down in sheets. We sat for quite some time watching the deluge. A pick-up truck arrived with a group of Thais on a Sunday excursion. The men sat in the driver's cab smoking while the women sat in the truck bed with only the flimsy protection of bits of cardboard held over their heads. Needless to say, they were completely soaked. The truck reversed under the *sala* roof to give the women a break. They all laughed and looked like they were having a ball. When the rain eventually eased off, the pick-up continued on its way and the women waved goodbye to the strange foreigners.

The peak of the rainy season occurs between August and September. Heavy rain falls more or less daily during the afternoons or evenings, with dramatic thunderstorms and lightning illuminating the sky in a stunning spectacle of nature's power. The water level in the rivers rises, and the lowlands often flood. Thais living in the rural areas are well prepared for this, as traditional houses are built upon poles. Except during years of exceptional rainfall, they are safe from any flooding.

A foreigner who isn't used to the monsoon doesn't accept the rain as stoically as a Thai. For instance, he won't accept rain coming through the roof and having to put buckets on the floor. Like us, our foreign neighbours at the mill were troubled with a leaking roof, and sought help from the caretaker to repair it. The reply was that he would check the roof once the rainy season was over. This was obviously of little comfort.

The roof of our own company house withstood the tropical downpours quite well, but we had a crack in the wall and an ill-fitting window through which the rains came to turn our floor into a big puddle. Finally, after Gunilla's persistent requests, the "engineer" turned up one day with a big tube of silicon paste. He smeared the paste into the crack in the wall. With the same energy, he also smeared it around the window frame and apologized when he got some on the glass. He immediately pulled out a rag and smeared the smudge over the whole window. He didn't exactly leave the tidiest job behind him, but at least our house was now dry.

Frogs leap about everywhere after a downpour, as if they had tumbled down with the rain, so we have to take great care not to trample on one when we step outside the door. If we open the window, we have to look out for leaf frogs jumping along the walls. Even though we are attentive in preventing a frog invasion of our house, one small devil managed to sneak in and sit on the edge of our bed one morning, waking us with his dawn performance. Gunilla soon expelled him out to his friends in the garden. In the evenings there is often a big frog concert, during which the different species display their incredible vocal prowess. Some frogs keep to the storm drains and get additional support from the good acoustics, providing a powerful bass line for the choir.

Water and drainage form a special chapter in the art of Thai home-keeping that can make a foreigner pull his hair out. We fought a losing battle against the plumbing for a long time. Gunilla eventually established a good working relationship with the neighbourhood's jack-

of-all-trades, who made several emergency repairs in our company house. One day, the water main broke and inundated the place. When it was fixed, there was a blockage in the drain instead. Water conduits usually consist of blue PVC pipes glued together. The technique for drainage has not evolved much from the traditional solution of putting a hole in

the wall where water can pour out. Drainage gave us trouble for a long time. When we emptied the dishwater in the kitchen sink, it ran back into the bathroom sink and out onto the floor.

The 'engineer'-cum-'plumber' finally turned up with his equipment and soiled the whole house to the point where Gunilla was on the verge of tears. At last he packed up, announced with a smile that he was done, and vanished. Gunilla turned on the tap in the bathroom sink and happily noted that the water disappeared down the plughole. Then she went into the kitchen and found where the water had gone.

The next day, Gunilla got hold of the man again. This time he smeared silicon sealant in all the places where he could see water pouring out. At last we got our kitchen into order and did our dishes, but suddenly Gunilla felt water flowing around her feet where she was standing at the sink. The man had to make yet another visit and smear on yet more silicon. Finally, no more water escaped and our floors were dry.

One rule for living in Thailand is to be friends with water in all its forms and, when necessary, use silicon sealant liberally as the cure-all.

12. In The World Of The Lord Buddha

It was not until we had been living in a country with a different cultural background that we came to realize how many of our conceptions and values have their origins in Christian traditions. Nor do we, as Swedes, often think about how much Luther's catechisms really dominate our habits. When, for example, we have not managed to complete all that we had planned for the day, we make up excuses about either enjoying life or being lazy.

Thais take a genuine interest in the message of the Lord Buddha. Monks participate actively in society. They conduct lessons in the schools. They officiate over family occasions, car purchases, and factory openings, giving their blessings by chanting religious texts. Students

show their respect by *wai*ing the Buddha statue in front of school at the end of each day. Families devote spare time to go on pilgrimages to renowned temples and to listen to reputable wise monks.

Many Thais wear small, gold-mounted Buddha amulets on thick, gold chains. They give the wearer a sense of security, so they are reluctant to take them off. I once went on a weekend excursion with my staff, snorkelling around the coral reefs off Koh Chang. One girl in our group found herself in a dilemma. Should she remove her amulet before throwing herself into the water? Finally, with great reverence, she pulled the chain over her head, held it in her hands, and made a pious *wai* before placing the amulet in her bag.

Temples in the countryside are gathering points for villagers, who help with the maintenance of the buildings. The beautifully-decorated ceremony hall, or *bot,* is what first draws attention. It is primarily intended for special meetings of the monks. Mosaic patterns, containing tiny mirror fragments, make it sparkle in the sun. Ornate, gilt mythological figures, *cho faa*, adorn the roof, their heads reaching for the sky.

A large, simple community hall, built on columns, is where the public ceremonies are held. There is also a bell tower and, for some, a crematorium with a high chimney. Distinguished temples which house relics also have a *stupa* or *chedi* on the grounds. The *chedi* is shaped like a tapered bell, rising above the neighbourhood like a church steeple would in the West.

In the countryside, the private living quarters for the monks resemble small wooden storehouses built on poles. The appearance of the temple and its surrounding buildings reflects the people's economic contribution and provides a rough gauge of the surrounding area's wealth.

In general, the Buddha's rules for living correspond to the Bible's Ten Commandments. The true Buddhist should not kill, steal, commit adultery, lie, or use intoxicating substances. But if, one day, he breaks one of these rules, he is only

responsible to himself, and need not be troubled with a bad conscience. The Buddhist can make up for his misdemeanour with good deeds on a later occasion.

Buddhism differs in one major regard from Christianity in that there is no God to be responsible to. It is totally up to the individual how he wishes to develop his spiritual condition in order to improve his next life. Performing kind deeds is part of the Buddhist tradition. These deeds are credited to people's 'spiritual account' (or karma), so that they may be reassured of a better existence in their future life. The Buddha's rules for living act only as a guide for leading a decent life. If difficulties arise, people can make deviations from their beliefs according to their own judgement, and may choose to resolve extreme problems through unconventional methods. For example, there is no difficulty in hiring a professional killer in Thailand. In exchange for reasonable remuneration, the assassin liquidates a client's competitor in political or business life. Politicians and successful businessmen surround themselves with bodyguards and often travel with a police escort when moving around the countryside.

Foreigners often find that the Thais have only modest confidence in laws and regulations. The attitude towards obeying laws and rules is considerably more flexible than what Westerners are used to; in Thailand it may be true to say that they are conceived more as a description of a desired condition rather than as definite rules. Even if people realize that they have committed an unacceptable act, they can later mitigate their offence with charitable deeds. A practicing Buddhist can continue to drink, hunt, steal, lie, kill, and visit the brothel, yet the very next day make a donation to the temple in his home village, or temporarily join the monkhood, and feel as if he has been absolved of wrongdoing.

Donations for charitable purposes are very common in Thailand. The Buddhist establishment is financed by gifts from the faithful who want to improve their karma and compensate for their lapses. The motive to do meritorious deeds probably doesn't have any determining importance. It is rather the accumulated sum of such deeds that counts for how successful people are in their everyday life, both in large ways and small. With many good deeds, people believe they can remain in good health, achieve economic success, and improve their social status.

There isn't any all-seeing supervisor to make sure that the spiritual rules are obeyed. The State issues laws and the police force does its best

to keep the citizens in order, but while Buddha has marked out the road to spiritual development, there is no spiritual authority.

The personal responsibility that is so evident in Buddhism is surely also a reason why the Thais are inveterate individualists. They want their own little businesses in the form of a small shop or a trading company. Co-operation is not a particularly well-developed Thai virtue. The confidence in their own ability is, on the other hand, sublime, and manifests itself in distrust and an unwillingness to follow advice and directions from others, particularly foreigners. This is a common frustration that Westerners, especially, meet in Thailand.

You can detect reflections of this behaviour far back in Siamese history. On a visit to the ancient Khmer ruins of Angkor in Cambodia, some of the stone reliefs illustrate a Khmer king's victory over his enemies, the Chams of Vietnam. The tour guide gave his own view of the Thai character. The Khmer troops march along in well-organized lines with their spears in perfect alignment. The Siamese auxiliary troops follow in a big disordered horde with their spears pointing in all directions. Not much has changed during the last 800 years.

Buddhism shows a great veneration towards nature, and it is sometimes described (along with Jainism) as the only religion that has an ecological view of life. A true Buddhist avoids harming any form of life, and a monk is not supposed to go outside at night for the risk of stepping onto some little creature that he can't see. It is all the more depressing to see how this Buddhist outlook is actually practiced in Thailand. Forty years ago, Thailand was, to a large extent, covered with forest. Today there are only some so-called 'protected' areas left. Mountains that up until recently were covered with green primeval forests look distressingly bare today. The Swedish clear-felling practice, when it was at its most extensive in the 1970s, can, in comparison to such deforestation, be considered as a mere thinning-out measure. The exploitation of much-sought-after tropical wood has been very efficient, and the commercial interests have not met any widespread resistance. Re-plantation has, until now, only been on a very unassuming scale, and the natural forest is being replaced with straight-lined plantations of non-native eucalyptus.

The driving forces in this so called 'development' are not directly involved in the devastation, but simply hire contractors to carry out their dirty work. In this way they do not break Buddhist principles themselves, and thus do not have to trouble themselves with a bad conscience. Why should they feel responsible for people that they have employed to cut down trees? Today there is still felling going on in the natural forests, and one can still buy a felling licence or in other ways exploit poor or greedy people's needs. I once read in one of the English-language dailies an open letter to the Forestry Department from a logging contractor. He was complaining about the big bribes he had to pay to different clerks to conduct his work, and how these steep charges made it difficult to make ends meet.

Thai society has found a strange balance between different interests. Pork and chicken are standard ingredients in Thai dishes. Monks, who are the representatives of the Buddha's teaching in society, happily fill themselves with pork, fish, and chicken. How does this fit? the average Westerner asks. As long as they don't do the killing themselves, then it is all right. There is always someone who, in return for an appropriate payment, will act as the butcher.

☙❧

Buddhist traditions remain evident all over Thailand, even though they seem to be at odds with the modern consumer society that Thais seem to desire insatiably. Lord Buddha taught that craving is the root cause of our suffering, and that by practicing meditation we should be able to discipline ourselves and turn our minds away from this world full of want. The message is just as relevant today as it was 2,500 years ago—perhaps even more so.

Most young men in Thailand ordain as Buddhist monks for a short period of time, and have the opportunity to practice meditation under the guidance of senior monks. This is an accepted reason for taking leave from one's workplace and is seen as an important rite of passage: an entrance ticket to becoming a full member of society. Women cannot ordain as 'nuns' in the Thai Buddhist world, but meditation training is available for everyone, provided by both Buddhist and non-Buddhist organizations throughout the country. It is a remarkable experience to see young men and women returning to work after they have spent some time in a Buddhist temple or meditation centre. There is often serenity in their faces reflecting a spiritual harmony.

Gunilla once enrolled in meditation training for ten days, and it was not without some anxiety that she departed for the retreat not far away from our home. There would be strict regulations to follow, particularly difficult for an energetic Westerner: no social contacts, no talking to other participants, and long meditation sessions sitting cross-legged and motionless on the floor. A *noble silence* would prevail during the whole stay. To start with, it was difficult just to overcome the pain from sitting cross-legged for hours on end. Gradually, with some degree of success, Gunilla managed to liberate her mind from her aching body and, for short periods, bring it to a state of harmony. But, by the end of the retreat, she was totally exhausted. When she returned home, she immediately let loose her craving for talking.

In her English teaching in local schools, Gunilla noticed a distinct difference in the childrens' ability to concentrate and stay attentive during classes. The children in one of the schools made much better progress than those in the other, in spite of the fact that the Thai teacher could hardly exchange a world of English with her. One day, Gunilla arrived early for her class at that school. It was the lunch break, but the yard was empty and the whole compound silent. At first she thought that she had missed some information about the school being closed for the day. Then she noticed the teacher sitting on the wide porch running along the school building. She went over to the porch and there, coming into view, she found the children sitting in rows practicing meditation.

Gunilla retreated and waited until the teacher finished the session. After becoming aware of this regular meditation practice during the lunch break in this school, Gunilla was convinced that this was the explanation for the good performance of these children.

The queen's birthday is also celebrated as Mother's Day in Thailand, and most children pay respect to their mothers and grandmothers on this day—but not in the way you find in many Western countries, with presents and cakes. Some children in the countryside go with the female members of their family to the temple, where they stay for a day or two in meditation. Both the children and the adults dress in white as they line up in front of the temple and are led inside by the monks. Grandmothers, mothers, and children sit down side by side on the floor and, guided by the monks, they turn their minds away from daily hardships in the fields or at school. Practicing meditation together on Mother's Day brings family members closer together and creates positive feelings. Many Thais also practice meditation regularly at home, and this habit very likely contributes to their overall patience and tolerance.

During the rainy season, all monks have to stay in their temple and devote themselves to their studies. When the rains stop, they are free to wander across the country. In October, the Kathin festival is when gifts are carried forward to the monks in the temples. We have participated in Kathin festivals in villages near the mill, when the company sponsors the ceremony and employees collect money for the temple. It is a big feast for the villagers, and the community hall is filled with people sitting on the floor. Carpets are spread out and big arrangements of orchids put around the Buddha statue. When you see village houses, you might think that their owners are poor, and compared to Western norms, village folk do live simply. On a day like this, however, the women are adorned in their best outfits and glittering golden chains.

Served with a glass of Coca-Cola, we sit down with the villagers before the Buddha statue and beneath a podium where the monks sit in a line. The ceremony starts with the monks chanting texts in Pali, the classical Indian language. Their monotonous 'song' creates a religious atmosphere. In the meantime, the devotees sit with palms held together before them, while gifts are laid out on a big table. When the chanting is over, the villagers carry the gifts out of the community hall.

A procession with long drums, electric guitar, and a big amplifying system on a bicycle-drawn cart is waiting outside. A group of dancing women takes the lead, followed by the blaring 'orchestra.' The retinue follows them, carrying all the gifts. They dance three times around the temple before returning to the community hall and the waiting monks. It is now time to bring forward all the gifts, and the villagers crawl on their knees to place them in front of the monks. New lengths of saffron fabric are standard presents on an occasion like this. Monetary gifts are pegged to a miniature tree, where the bills hang like leaves. As a representative of the company, I assist in handing over gift-baskets: yellow plastic buckets, elegantly wrapped in orange cellophane, filled with all kinds of necessities like soap, toothpaste, and canned fruit. A monk then blesses the congregation by walking around the room and sprinkling holy water on one and all.

A Thai get-together is impossible without food. During the ceremony, the women cook at one end of the hall, and after the gifts have been handed out, they lay out the feast in front of the monks. After the monks have had their fill, the food is rearranged on the floor for everyone else to partake. People gather around the bowls in groups, and soon a nice party is in full swing. Elderly ladies open small baskets and pull out the ingredients for chewing betel, and soon they are busily chewing, chattering away, and enjoying the occasion to the full. Gunilla and I leave the community hall and step, sated and pleased, out into the blazing sun, where we are met by a blaring loudspeaker commenting on a soccer game on the temple's field outside the compound. We go home on our motorbike and hope that we have improved our karma somewhat for our next lives.

Sometimes the villagers arrange temple fairs, known as *ngaan wat*, that transform the temple grounds into a noisy festival and market-place with tents and vendors of all kinds. The main theme for the party might be religious, but this is relegated to the background behind the entertainment and commerce. The road to the temple fair is lined with welcoming yellow Buddhist flags, and red-white-and blue Thai flags. Fields around the temple are transformed into car parks, where pick-up trucks sit in long rows. People, dressed up for the occasion, come flocking to the site, where huge loudspeakers blare music and announcements. The fumes from all the cooking pots hang like a fog.

On entry to the grounds, one can buy a little package containing necessities for the Buddhist ritual: candles, incense sticks, a lotus flower, and a little sheet of gold-leaf foil. Just inside the walls, a monk sits under a canopy. He gives the kneeling visitors his blessing by sprinkling holy water with a big twig 'broom.' Worshippers light their candles and incense sticks, place the lotus flowers, and rub their small pieces of gold leaf onto the Buddha statue.

After that, the other attractions are awaiting. You can have your future told on a big wheel of fortune, or buy tickets to win teddy bears and boxes of chocolate. A travelling theatre group starts up their show behind the temple. The lavishly costumed actors perform a farcical open-air play, called *likay*, accompanied by a loud traditional orchestra.

Theatre speakers compete with Thai pop music from the market stalls, and it is a real party for the families as they stroll around. The children hold balloons in their hands and everyone munches on grilled chicken or other tasty snacks.

☙❦

Thais take a true interest in their friends' well-being, and it's not because of curiosity. Compassion is a true Buddhist virtue. In Thailand you share happy and sad events with both your family and friends, and others who may not be so close. Gunilla and I are sometimes invited to big wedding parties and funerals, and with our presence we honour the family concerned. By attending funerals you express your sympathy with the family and honour the deceased. It's more or less a social obligation, even if you don't know the deceased personally. In the beginning, I found it strange to receive such invitations from people with whom I had not had very close contacts. Gradually I understood the importance of participating in these social events. Weddings and funerals are not just small family gatherings, but often hundreds or even thousands of people are invited. Having some high-ranking people in attendance brings extra status to the family. These events can be a heavy financial burden to the family, but the guests are expected to give a donation in an envelope upon arrival, and a good wedding party may even provide a considerable surplus.

Even though funerals are not happy gatherings, you seldom find any open expression of sorrow, and there are few tears rolling down the cheeks. The Thais are masters at controlling their feelings in situations like this.

When one of the family members of the company owner passed away, impressive funeral rites were arranged in the evening for seven days, so that all employees could have the opportunity to pay their respects.

One of my managers came to me one day and asked for permission to go with most of the department staff to a funeral in Bangkok. Only a small group was left in the factory to carry out the most essential work. The mother of one of the staff had suddenly passed away, and now everyone in the department wanted to attend the funeral. A bus had already been arranged and was waiting for departure. What can a foreign manager do when faced with a case like this? Of course, you give your staff permission and ask them to convey your condolences to the family. At the same time, you hope that they will soon return and resume work.

One morning, a message arrived that a company commuter bus had been involved in a collision on its way to the mill, and several of the staff had been injured. Soon, a convoy of cars filled with employees left for the provincial hospital, where some of their friends were being treated for their injuries.

Sometimes, members of my staff also consult me in personal matters. Most of them are quite young, their parents far away, and I find myself acting as a surrogate father. After working in the company for a couple of years, the initial enthusiasm at having a job and a salary every month dissipates, and young people start thinking about the future. Should they be loyal to the company and patiently wait for promotion opportunities? What about higher education and the possibilities afforded by a master's degree? For the young women, the biggest dilemma is between career and motherhood. I was even asked by one girl if I thought it would be a good idea for her to get pregnant or not.

A young, very attractive woman in the company had difficulties dealing with the attentions of many of the men around her at work. She already had a boyfriend, but there were also other young men who were both attractive and attracted to her. She didn't really know whom to choose, and she was in despair. She considered resigning from the company and going back to her parents, who lived in the far north of Thailand, in order to escape from all the potential suitors. Her supervisor had observed the situation for some time and had a serious discussion with her. It was decided that it would not be a good solution to just run away from the problems and seek comfort from her parents. That would only cause them anxiety, as well. The supervisor instead recommended that she take a break from the mill and spend a week in a temple, where she could get guidance from senior monks regarding her life situation and relations with men. Meditation would also help her to gain a more objective view on her life. After this retreat she should come back to work and decide herself what she wanted to do with her life. The eventual outcome was that she left the company to continue her studies.

13. **Spirits And Gods**

Belief in ghosts and spirits is universal in Thailand. Spirits, especially, have to have somewhere to live, and one comes across charming miniature houses on pedestals everywhere in Thailand.

Thais believe that Nature is filled with spirits that can interfere with human life for better or for worse. Thus it is important to keep on good terms with them. If you have been prosperous, it is probably through the assistance of the spirit world, and you should show your gratitude with an appropriate offering at a site where a spirit lives.

Besides man-made spirit houses, trees are appropriate dwellings for spirits, and some are adorned with flowers, incense, and food. One often sees trees in Thailand wrapped with sashes of cloth and decorated in a similar way to the spirit houses. It is sometimes the case that a person who has won the first prize in a lottery attributed his luck to this particular special tree. Naturally, this tree will soon become a popular site for others with a burning desire to cash in on the lottery.

Since Buddhism does not demand the worship of divinities, there is nothing that stands in the way of reconciling your good standing in the spirit world with your Buddhist faith. Spirit houses are physically inhabited by little figures: a whole menagerie of animals and human or mythological characters; a Buddha image; or Indian gods like Brahma and Vishnu. The Thais display an unparalleled imagination and flexibility in their worship. The spirits are shown great veneration, but none of this has anything whatsoever to do with Buddhism. It is animism, Thai style.

Every large hotel or office building accommodates a spirit shrine, and on one weekend excursion we witnessed a hotel spirit being served breakfast. A waitress came out of the kitchen carrying a breakfast tray with little dishes, and approached the spirit house in a dignified manner. She laid out some fruit and a bowl of rice soup in front of the spirit

house before kneeling, bowing deeply, and making a *wai*. Then she returned to the kitchen. A cat had been sitting watching the morning ritual, and no sooner had the girl disappeared than it landed with an elegant leap on the spirit's breakfast table and contentedly lapped up the rice soup.

In the countryside, the spirits are treated in a less refined manner, adapted to their rural nature. When construction of the mill came to its most labour-intensive stage, it looked like a hurricane had ripped through the inside of the building. Welding wires lay like webbing across the floor, and fitters were perched like pigeons on rickety bamboo scaffolding high up in the ceiling. The working environment was not safe, even by Thai standards. One day, when I was passing through the main hall, I was totally taken aback. A large, plain table designated for displaying machinery blueprints had been cleared to accommodate a meal instead. In the middle of the table a big pig's head took centre stage surrounded by a number of other dishes and a large assortment of beer and local whiskey bottles. I was ready to run for help to prevent a party in the middle of the day, but kept my cool and asked a colleague what was going on. He explained that the feast was meant to improve the safety of the workplace. The factory spirit was to be given these treats so it would keep an eye out for any dangers. Roasted pig's head and whiskey were apparently the spirit's favourite treats. A worker poured some melted wax on the table, stood candles in place as it solidified, and lit them. He then fell to his knees in front of the pig's head with a bunch of incense sticks pressed between his palms.

Obviously the spirit of the factory was impressed by this splendid repast, because the machines were then assembled without serious mishap.

Construction in Thailand does not follow the same system as in Europe. Pre-made concrete elements are rarely used; instead, most concrete is poured into moulds that are made on the spot. In the beginning, I wasn't very impressed with the accuracy of this method. For instance, a flight of stairs had steps at different heights and angles. When I pointed out this apparent lack of care, I received a blank expression in response. Everything was, you see, totally in order and done on purpose—to prevent evil spirits from climbing the stairs. The adaptability of the spirits is limited, so they would thus inevitably trip over steps of different heights and tumble backwards.

Despite our attention to the spirits, disturbances occurred once production started. It proved difficult to reach the planned production volume; workers had accidents; and a fire caused huge damage to some of the machinery. It was again time to placate the spirit world and ask for help. The company's PR department was responsible for the arrangements, and a set of appropriate spirit dishes was ordered from the hotel. Another roasted pig's head was, of course, the main item. A collapsible table was erected in the factory and the meal laid out, together with drinks. The factory management lined up in front of the table and lit candles, which were then placed around the food. Incense sticks were handed out to the whole gathering, and everyone went up to light their sticks from the candles and place them in a pot of sand. After that, they knelt or bent their heads and called upon the protection of the spirit. The appeals were not responded to immediately after the ceremony, but eventually work started to go better, and the spirit seemed to have adjusted to its new environment.

☙❦❧

When a person dies in a traffic accident, his spirit becomes detached from his body and lingers by the scene of the trauma. Relatives provide a dwelling for the deceased's spirit by building a small spirit house. It is not a pleasant experience to die in a car crash, and so the lingering spirit also threatens other traffic at the site of the accident. Not until there has been a new accident at the same place will the first spirit experience peace and move on to a new life. People try to persuade the spirits at the site to avoid causing new accidents by leaving spirit houses decorated with wreaths of flowers. In spite of trying to keep the spirits in good spirits, more accidents inevitably occur at the same location, and so there can be whole groups of little houses along accident black spots where the angry spirits succeed each other as a continual threat to the passing traffic.

Belief in the spirit world feels very strange to some foreigners, but it is an accepted fact of life for Thais. Showing a condescending or ridiculing attitude toward the veneration of spirits makes it hard to gain the trust of any Thai. You need a humble attitude toward the supernatural to live successfully in Thai society.

Different Indian gods such as Brahma and Vishnu were worshipped before Buddhism became the dominant religion in Siam. Southeast Asia was heavily influenced by India on one side and China on the other. Even though Buddhism has been the official 'religion' for centuries, and the king its patron, Indian religious traditions still live on. There is a deep need, in different stages of Thai life, to seek the protection of a divine being. Buddhism has not been able to fulfill this need and, for certain events, a Brahmin ceremony is conducted in addition to, or in place of, the Buddhist ceremony.

This is especially so on occasions like weddings or foundation ceremonies for new buildings, since the god Brahma is the creator of the world and can thus bring to the participants fertility and a prosperous future.

The Thai wedding ceremony usually starts at dawn, with a general blessing of the couple and the congregation by Buddhist monks. It is important to be clear here that the Thai wedding ceremony is not a Buddhist ceremony, since Buddhism does not officially recognize marriage. The monks are invited simply to provide an opportunity for general merit-making and blessings on this auspicious occasion.

As with the Kathin ceremony, the monks sit in a line facing the congregation. A ball of cotton thread is untied and held in the hands of the monks. The monks then chant from Pali scriptures. As their voices rise and fall in the monotonous tones, the atmosphere created is mystical, almost bewitching. The rest of the participants sit attentively, silent, looking devout with their palms held together in front of them.

Very occasionally a Brahmin element may be introduced to the Thai wedding ceremony. This Brahmin ceremony often takes place later in the day, and leaves a light and positive impression. The Brahmin priest and his assistants are merry men with generous smiles, dressed in white leggings and tunics. During the ceremony, the assistants strike cymbals and perform fanfares with big conch shells. The priest and his assistants put on something of a show, but of course it is a serious ritual in which the priest, before an 'altar' covered in flowers, asks Brahma to give blessings for the future.

The Brahmin ceremony also contains many symbolic elements that are tailored for the event. The young couple are 'tied together' with a white cotton thread that circles both their heads, and items that represent their future life together are placed in their hands: a few eggs, bananas, small parcels of banana leaves with cooked rice. The items are blessed by the Brahmin priest, if he is present.

The Thai wedding ritual can seem rather shallow to a foreigner, with its noticeable emphasis on material wealth, but this suits the Thais just fine. One climax of the ceremony is when the bridegroom's dowry tray is carried in and blessed. On the tray, a box filled with gold jewellery is surrounded by piles of banknotes—some of which may be lent by relatives to help put on an impressive display.

❦

Before you can start the construction of any building in Thailand, you first have to arrange a foundation ceremony. It is appropriate to ask a Brahmin priest to participate, and to receive the blessing of Brahma. For a large building like a paper-mill, this can be quite a complicated ritual. A big box is filled with sand, placed on the ground at the site of the foundation, and draped with white cloth in a carefully pleated arrangement. After the priest's invocation to Brahma, the guests of honour gather around the sand box, where officials hold up big parasols as protection against the sun. Girls in neat office attire carry forward on gold-plated trays the ceremonial foundation poles made out of giltwood sticks. After the priest has blessed the sticks, the guests of honour get to knock them into the sand with a golden hammer. A beautiful marble plaque with a golden inscription is carried forward and placed on top of the sticks. The rest of the participants take a handful of petals from a

golden pot that the girls bring forward. They spread the petals over the marble plaque and it is soon hidden beneath a fragrant blanket. After such a foundation ceremony, workers can tackle the most complicated building project with confidence, assured that Brahma will keep an eye on their progress.

According to Eastern traditions, there is a lot of magic associated with numbers and number combinations. Thus you have to pay attention to such matters if you want to be successful. Numerology is almost considered a science, and is taken very seriously. The figure nine is special. Ceremonial items surrounding the king are usually nine in number. For example, at royal ceremonies, officials carry a parasol with nine tiers.

A day such as September 9th, 1999 was an occasion that couldn't pass by unnoticed. According to the Thai newspapers, many pregnant women went to hospitals to have their babies delivered prematurely by Caesarean section on that day—even though the Thai Buddhist calendar is about 500 years ahead of the Western calendar. A child could become especially prosperous as a result, and parents couldn't let such an opportunity slip by. On this same morning, a ceremony was arranged in our company in front of the little Brahmin temple outside the administration building, and at 9:09 precisely, employees came flocking to light nine incense sticks each, that were placed in a pot in front of the all-seeing god with his four faces.

◑✝◐

With the arrival of a modern industrial society in Thailand, prevalent animistic beliefs have moved onto the factory floor with the young engineers who operate the machinery. According to the workers in our mill, it seems that the spirits occupying the production space are true masculine characters. What I didn't bargain on is that the male spirits really like to protect their territory from female influences.

In my technical department I have several female engineers, who I assign now and then to carry out process studies. After completion of these studies, we normally review the findings and make our conclusions together. One project required the close monitoring of one particular machine's operating performance, and one of the female engineers, Jiap, had been assigned to this job. When I asked her later about her observations, she said that it was difficult to see clearly from the control room, but she had got all the necessary information from some of the male operators. At first I got annoyed at this, believing that she was afraid of

smearing her uniform on the dirty machine. However, the explanation was totally unexpected. The machine crew, consisting only of men, did not allow any women near the machine. It seems they had an agreement with the influential factory spirit to keep women away from the machine in exchange for trouble-free operation. It was okay for a female engineer to stay in the control room and make observations from there, but not anywhere closer to the machine.

I asked Jiap why she had not asked the supervisor for assistance, but he too was a slave to the whims of the spirit. In order to make Jiap feel better about the situation, I told her that I would discuss this unacceptable behaviour with the department manager so she could do her job without interference the next time. Unfortunately, Jiap did not think this would be of any help, because the manager supported the whole operating team in their relations with the spirit world. In a situation like this, a foreigner is totally lost, and the scientific approach I had tried to introduce for process studies had been ignored.

☙❦❧

The Thais have an uncanny ability to take on traditions and ideas from different cultures and mix them together into a Thai cocktail that fills their spiritual and social needs. This process of incorporating new cultures has been going on for centuries, and still continues in a dramatic way. Western traditions are now being adopted, and commercialism has a massive influence on Thai society today. The result is an odd combination of traditional Thai values and modern Western practices. Just witness how Thailand's rabid consumerism reaches fever pitch around Christmas and New Year. I get the feeling that it won't be long until the Indian divinity Ganesh, who sits permanently in the spirit house outside some shopping centres, will soon be exchanged for a beaming Santa Claus during the Christmas season, and indeed the entire year round.

14. Wisdom And Beauty

Before all important planned events in Thailand, one should consult an astrologer to be sure that the stars are in a favourable position. To officially open a factory or get married without assuring oneself of celestial blessings is downright irresponsible. There are numerous examples of how disastrous things can turn out if one doesn't consult an astrologer—and not only in Thailand. A recent case in point is the new Chek Lap Kok Airport in Hong Kong. When the air traffic control office was moved over to the new airport, chaos ensued. The air traffic controllers had to promptly return to the old airport for a transitional period. In this case they had not taken advice from an astrologer. They had, for instance, given the new airport a name that went against Chinese tradition. An airport name should not have more than eight letters.

Chinese traditions are deeply ingrained in Thai society and have melded with traditional Thai customs. The collective knowledge of Thai astrologers is based on Chinese observations thousands of years old that cannot easily be dismissed. Once, a Thai tried to convince me of the validity of the application of this knowledge to modern society by giving me an example that a foreigner could understand. According to Chinese tradition, you should not build a house on the far side of a T-junction. Chinese through the millennia have always been in too much of a hurry with their rickshaws; hurtling straight through a T-junction and into the house of some imprudent homeowner was an all-too-common occurence. It is on such empirical observations that Chinese wisdom is based, whereas the uninformed foreigner might be inclined to dismiss this knowledge as superstition.

I objected to this example and pointed out that a new dormitory building was at a T-junction a few kilometres from the factory. But there is always a Thai solution to such a problem—they simply erected a magnificent spirit house at the crossroads. With the help of the spirit

當敢石山泰

world, they could ward off nightly speeders from driving smack into the middle of the building. Strange that the Chinese didn't think of that.

No astrology-based mistakes were made during the construction of our mill. An astrologer was consulted well in advance for the best time to commence operations. The day for the official opening was set, and work began immediately to complete construction before the opening date. However, the project-management team realized soon enough that the mill couldn't possibly be finished by the proposed date. There would be no paper production because important systems would not be operational in time.

But it was impossible to put back the day of the opening. Even though the factory would not be fully operational as planned, a major effort was still made to arrange the grandiose opening ceremony. The area around the factory, littered with scattered building materials, was cleaned up with incredible efficiency. The muddy roads with water-filled potholes were neatly paved, and footpaths were laid alongside them. The fields around the mill, which had turned into quagmires during the rainy season, wet enough for rice planting, were now leveled and turfed. Any remaining building materials left behind were simply covered over by the turf.

On the morning of the opening day, the mill area had been transformed from a construction site into a pleasant park, resplendent with fluttering flags, suitable for the pomp of the opening ceremony. When the guests of honour arrived, the staff was lined up along the roads in their new company uniforms and white hard hats. The new machinery had been decorated with banners in the colours of the Thai flag, and a brass band was playing fanfares which echoed around the factory walls. It was an impressive sight for the guests who had the honour of pressing the button that officially started paper production. After a few seconds of intense anticipation, some parts of the machine slowly started to move, and the assembly applauded enthusiastically. The guests of honour and their entourage inspected the rest of the plant. The factory was now opened on the set day, and the work to complete construction could continue.

During construction, office premises were in small, temporary cabins located in muddy fields. Impatient with delays, we watched the office construction slowly progress. Finally it was time to leave the cabins behind and move into the brand new office building. I asked my staff to start shifting the next day. But, it wasn't that simple, of course. First we had to set an appropriate moving day by consulting a local astrologer. Luckily, we didn't have to wait too long: there was a propitious full moon the very next week.

The entrance to the mill grounds is of a grand design. A long, four-lane road, flanked by trees and well-manicured flower-beds, leads straight to the mill. One is greeted by the impressive view of the power plant with its giant chimney. Before one approaches the office buildings, there is a junction with a service road leading off. Delivery trucks use the service road on both incoming and outgoing trips. They have to be weighed on the weighbridge in the service road before being admitted into the delivery area, and then again on the way out. If you continue on the service road, you pass an artificial lake with red water lilies, just behind the office buildings. After yet another curve, and another junction, there is another entrance into the mill.

The entrance road that leads directly to the mill was blocked at an early stage, and all the traffic was re-directed by the company's security guards to the service road. This detour puzzled employees as well as

visitors, and soon came to be a source of irritation for all. A lengthy queue often formed in front of the weighbridge on the service road. Many employees ignored the barricades and found new ways to get to work. To end these short cuts, the company's security service barricaded the original entrance more effectively with large freight containers. The company's management refused to give any explanation for the barricades, insisting that the employees should learn to follow rules and not question the company's decisions.

There was much speculation about this. At one stage, a rumour circulated that it was the pond that was at the centre of the mystery. According to Chinese tradition, a detour around a body of water would have an advantageous effect on people's minds. Perhaps the extra bend around the pond was meant to be a way of clearing one's mind before starting the day's work. The resourcefulness of employees is always evident when they are working around incomprehensible regulations, and soon many had found new routes around the container barrier. The countermove from the company didn't take long. The security guards now had extended powers to stop those errant employees and report them to the security manager.

The employees got more and more heated with the situation, and the matter was discussed at a meeting with the company's management. Several employees bravely questioned the strange traffic regulation. They wanted an explanation that would motivate them to actually follow the rules. The chairman looked very severe when he announced that it was a policy decision. When he was asked if it was possible to change a policy that no one understood, he was speechless. Another Thai intervened and stated that it was a Chinese belief that was the basis for the decision. At this stage, the Western participants wondered aloud what Chinese belief could possibly lead to a newly constructed entrance road being blocked off by freight containers. Finally, with a certain effort, an explanation was given. The high chimney of the power plant was the stumbling block.

As a Western technocrat, I find a tall industrial chimney an impressive sight, but obviously the Chinese have a very different opinion. Such an 'eyesore' is considered a bad omen when people drive up to the mill. In the Buddhist world, the deceased are cremated, and some temples also have a crematorium—with a tall chimney. It was a big error in the planning of the mill, now 'corrected' by the seemingly strange re-direction of traffic. One simply couldn't let people enter the grounds as if it were an invitation to a funeral. Such things can cause unforeseeable damage to one's spiritual well-being and, more importantly, the profit margins of the company. The entrance had to be re-built so that the high chimney didn't darken the horizon, or our minds, on the way in to

work. Running an industrial business in Asia is a complex task. Apart from the technical, market, and economic issues, people also have to take into account beliefs based on ancient traditions.

One of these beliefs is referred to as *feng shui*, the very complex ancient 'science' of energy flow and positive and negative forces, Yin and Yang, that interact with the elements of Nature. Opposing elements such as fire and water must not be positioned so that negative energy is created. If this happens, it is still possible to overcome bad *feng shui* by artificial means, to avoid disasters in one's family and business. Metal freight containers, it seemed, could create the necessary barrier to separate a negative force from people on their way to work in the morning.

In Thailand, entrances to factories—as well as to temples and official institutions— are designed with great care. They are lined with beautiful lawns and shrubberies, imposing gates, and expensive signs, preferably in polished stone and embossed with the organization's name in gold letters. It is all designed to impress visitors. Behind the magnificent façades are hidden utilitarian office buildings and messy factory areas.

Thai society aspires to create a beautiful façade, even if what lies behind it is not that impressive. This goes not only for buildings; Thais also describe other phenomena in terms of praise that go far beyond reality. To a Thai, this seems totally natural. When I objected to the design of an information leaflet about our company, in which the mill was described as the most advanced of its kind in the world, I received the reply that this was an advertising brochure and it was supposed to elaborate on the truth a little.

This kind of embellishment is standard practice in Thailand, and one encounters it everywhere. Soon, we Westerners took a rather sceptical view. Factory premises are designed in a rather Spartan way, except for those areas where visitors are allowed to view the working environment. An interior designer gives these areas an elegant touch, and so these parts of the premises take on a rather fantastic character, with chrome-plated panels, glass walls, and spotlights arranged to emphasize certain products and details of the production process. Specific paths convey guests through the factory, and great care is taken to ensure that these areas are neat and tidy. These areas are scrubbed and even re-painted when distinguished guests are expected.

The Thai language has a way of expressing certain ideas that do not easily translate into English. An English translation for a Thai's positive comments becomes an exercise in superlatives. Restaurants happily describe their menus as "luxurious dreams for the exclusive gourmet"; hotels promise "heavenly experiences"; property developers describe their new condominium projects as "the ultimate of elite lifestyle." And so on. Never mind the garbled English, anyone who falls for such advertising can be disappointed when he finds a much more modest reality.

On one occasion I was asked to write a draft for a press release regarding an agreement on technical co-operation that our company had entered into with a Western company. I drafted what I thought was a balanced description of what this co-operation would mean for our company. I realized, of course, that I had to slant the material so that the positive results were clearly emphasized. I sent my draft to our PR department for review, and when I got it back it had been re-written to the point where I could barely recognize it. The agreement was now described as "revolutionary" to Thai industry, one that would give Thailand "a technological advantage over all competitors." I contacted the PR department and asked them why they had distorted my text. They told me that they had had to re-write it into what they called "Thai newspaper style."

One also experiences over-embellishment in product descriptions. Every now and then, I got to proofread material that went on the packaging of our paper. The marketing department's descriptions usually dumbfounded me. The wrappings promised "faultless functioning in all kinds of conditions" and "the highest quality workmanship." For paper! Sometimes they also wanted to emphasize that the products were certified ISO9001 (the standard for Quality Management Systems) and ISO14001 (the standard for Environmental Management).

I told the marketing and advertising people that what they wanted to print on the packaging was bordering on misrepresentation. We were hardly able to make the guarantees that they were claiming. We also had to be especially careful if the products were to be exported to the West, where people have a different view of what is "faultless" and "highest quality." The text on the wrappings was, of course, just a way to promote sales.

When you do formal presentations to your bosses in Thailand, you have to be strategic and select suitable facts, and present them in a straightforward, easy-to-understand fashion. Avoid the negative. You need to call attention to the positive changes that you have brought about. In Thai companies, you are now and then requested to make a formal presentation to your superiors about your work achievements and how you have contributed to the success of the company. Thais are adept at this, and use computers to embellish their presentations, with PowerPoint images flashing over the projection screen in a beautiful slideshow. This usually impresses the company management, even though real performance may have been very modest. I sometimes get the feeling that the colours of the three dimensional bars in the graphs on these screens are more important than the height of the bars themselves.

An avarage Westerner might consider this kind of presentation as an opportunity to air the difficulties he has identified and how he would like to introduce improvements for the betterment of the company. He would not stay up all night in front of the computer to make colourful, moving images. Instead, he would note down summarized bullet points and present these with the help of the more traditional overhead projector. It is easy to figure out which style of presentation scores the most points with Thai management.

15. School

Before we moved to Thailand, Gunilla had been working for 25 years as a pre-school and Montessori teacher in Sweden. Curious about how teaching was conducted in the Thai countryside, she visited the school in a village near the mill. This is a typical rural school: kindergarten to grade six. The school buildings lie in the shade of large trees by a sports field. The temple stands on the opposite side. Classrooms are lined up beside each other, entrances facing a long covered porch that runs the length of the schoolhouse. The doors are always left open to let air flow through the classrooms. Big ceiling fans are always whirling, as well. The mandatory flagpole stands in front, and each morning the children line up in the yard to pay respect to the nation, the monarchy, and the religion. The pre-school department is in a separate building: it's a big, single room lacking any furniture except for the teacher's desk. The children carry out their exercises sitting on the floor, just as they do at home. When they move up to the first grade, at the age of seven, they get to sit on a chair.

It is compulsory to wear the school uniform in Thai schools, and even the smallest pre-school children arrive wearing their white shirts and khaki-coloured shorts or blue skirts. The expense for uniforms can be burdensome for parents in the countryside. Thus clothes are passed down among siblings, and the youngest have to make do with patched and threadbare blouses, once white, that are now dingy grey. Even if you can read Thai, you cannot assume that the name embroidered on the blouse is correct, because it might well be the name of an elder sister.

A female teacher is in charge of fifty children between the age of three and seven in the pre-school department. She has a completely different role compared with her Swedish counterparts. In Thailand, the teacher is an authoritarian figure who keeps a distance from the children. As her assistant, she has a thin cane to punish young troublemakers. The miscreant who might have stolen or destroyed something puts his or her hand forward to receive a caning. It is a virtue to not show any

emotion, and punished children seldom emit a sound, even if their eyes are watering and teardrops roll silently down their cheeks. It is not an emotionless relationship, though, as the teacher does care about the children—but no child would ever get the idea to give their teacher a hug, as is the case in Sweden.

Gunilla realized, on her first visit, that she would be able to make a contribution in this pre-school, and she later spent three mornings a week with the class. She took on a different role from an ordinary teacher, of course. Gunilla sat on the floor with the children, while the teacher sat at her desk. Older children approached her with their notebooks to get help with writing the tricky English letters. At first, the children were rather shy in front of the strange foreign 'teacher' who didn't behave like a proper teacher at all. Eventually, though, their fear dissolved and Gunilla was quite well liked by the children. They would sit close to her and, once in a while, give her a hug.

It was as strange for Gunilla to adjust to this environment as it was for the little three-year-olds left by their parents outside. Gunilla couldn't help but worry about one little girl who, in the beginning, refused to enter the classroom and remained seated outside on the stairs with her knapsack on her back, crying. The Thai teacher didn't seem to worry, so Gunilla asked her what was wrong with the girl. The answer was both unexpected and obvious: "She is only three years old, and longs for her mother." Aside from this, the teacher regarded the child's distress as natural, and seemed not to take any further notice of the girl. In Europe, parents and teachers would have mollycoddled the girl for however long it took.

After one week of crying in protest, the girl took off her knapsack and moved into the classroom, where she soon started to play with the other children. The process of adjusting to school in Thailand is not the same as it is in Sweden. In Western society, we want to protect our children from all emotional distress, and feel bad if we expose them to unhappiness. A Thai child is probably more prepared to meet distress as an adult.

To start with, the range of activities available to pre-school children was very limited. The older children learned their letters and counting, while the younger ones occupied themselves with simple plastic toys. The teacher was mostly busy at her desk and had little time to attend to the younger ones. The class had a desperate need for activity, and so Gunilla started to introduce more things to do. One involved teaching the children to wash their blouses, and it soon came to be one of their favourite occupations. Children all over the world love to splash water about, and here they got to do this and some practical work at the same time.

The children experienced something totally new when Gunilla taught them how to paint with watercolours. They started with small, cautious daubs, but soon many developed into little artists and depicted their surroundings: houses on poles, palm trees, rice fields, and a big sun in the sky. They always painted the sun red, which may seem a little

strange. In the middle of the day, when all Thais sensibly stay indoors or take a nap in the shade, the sun is white-hot and something to avoid. In the late afternoon and early evening, though, when Thais emerge from indoors to socialize, the sun approaches the horizon and transforms itself into a big red ball.

Many of the children had never seen a jigsaw puzzle before, and they turned and twisted the bits enthusiastically to put together exciting scenes from *The Jungle Book* and other cartoons. The girls struggled

valiantly with small weaving frames and proudly carried home the little bags that Gunilla had helped them to make. Gunilla wished that she had at least eight arms, like an octopus, to help all these children with such a stifled need for intellectual stimulation.

When the children turn seven, they move up to the big school. Rural teaching methods are not very advanced, and the education level of the teachers isn't high. The teacher stands in front of the blackboard reading out loud, and then the children repeat in chorus. There is never any direct dialogue; the children learn by rote. They start learning English in first grade, and the teachers try the best they can with their very limited knowledge by reading aloud from the textbook. The children never get to hear proper English pronunciation, either on audio tape, TV, or from native speakers, and it is easy to understand why many Thais struggle to speak English well: they never get to listen to the language. The classroom vocabulary may be acceptable, but forming new sentences and ideas beyond the content of the textbook used at school is outside the curriculum. On TV, all foreign programmes are dubbed, and Japanese samurais and Chicago gangsters incongruously speak fluent Thai.

The Thai expression for classroom training, *aan nang seua*, also reflects the way teaching is conducted. You literally 'read from the book' and the students are expected to repeat verbatim after the teacher. Teachers don't have to be very familiar with the subject they are teaching, as long as they can recite the text and the children are being attentive.

Besides assisting in kindergarten classes, Gunilla has also contributed with English teaching in the sixth grade, where the children have already had basic English education for some years. The teacher was very happy to have someone who could speak English to assist him in the classroom. To start with, it was difficult for Gunilla to understand what the school wanted her to do because of the teacher's limited English ability. It soon became obvious, however, that the children were in desperate need of developing their speaking skills because they had never had anyone to practice with. Gunilla put the textbook away and conducted her classroom hours in a totally different way, with the children interacting with her and their friends in a more active way.

In order to give the children an example of the practical use of English, Gunilla started a pen-pal club with a school in Sweden. This was a new experience for the children, and it was a very exciting day when the first batch of letters was received from the Swedish children. Of course, both sets of 12-year-olds wrote about their immediate environments and their daily lives. But it was two different worlds that were described in this exchange of letters. The Swedish children wrote about their well-furnished rooms equipped with TV and computer, and how they enjoyed skiing in the mountains with their parents during the winter holidays. The Thai kids, on the other hand, described their families and how they got up at dawn to help their mothers with their younger siblings and to iron their uniforms before going to school. In almost all the Thai letters, the children also explained how they loved their parents and the school. It is hard to say how the two groups of children on opposite sides of the globe perceived the environment of their pen pals, but it was a true cultural collision.

Teachers are very relaxed in spite of their authoritarian role. They often sit at their desk reading a newspaper, or walk on the verandah outside the classroom, smoking with their colleagues. Once a week it is compulsory for them to wear their civil servant's uniform. The uniforms are khaki and bear badges of rank and ribbons announcing various honours. It is easy to get the impression of a military institution.

The female principal looks like a general with her golden epaulettes. The uniform emphasizes the position of the school staff, which gives them a certain status in society, though they can barely survive on their meagre salaries.

The children participate in cleaning the school in a way that is not done in the West. They have to sweep the school rooms and scrub the toilets. At lunchtime, the older pupils prepare the food under the supervision of a teacher. As usual in Thai cooking, a lot of vegetables have to be chopped before ending up in the big wok.

The children usually bring their own rice. The school lunch is served in an open-sided room. After the meal, the children take care of the dishes. Stray dogs, waiting patiently at a distance, quickly move in to snap up any leftovers.

The government recently created an investment scheme, granting schools the funds to purchase computers. The village school now has a computer room where the children can practice their English. It is questionable how effective this is, but it is probably better than nothing. Who got the most out of this deal was most likely the company that had close contacts with the education minister and got the contract to provide Thailand's schools with the computers.

The knowledge taught in the village school is rather rudimentary, but compulsory school attendance has been extended to nine years. Village children go by bus to the senior-level schools in the district capital. The teachers' level of education must be raised to give children a better foundation for their integration into modern society. The new industries have totally different demands from those of the traditional agricultural society, and the rural Thai education system has still not caught up. When young people eventually get jobs in the new factories, the shortcomings of the educational system are revealed. They particularly lack initiative and problem-solving ability. This is not so strange when you consider that teachers have always told pupils what to do, and children have never had the opportunity to question or to solve a problem for themselves.

When we started our departmental meetings in the mill, I found it difficult at first to engage staff in discussion. I initially put this down to the language barrier, but discovered the same reticence even when a Thai manager was conducting the meeting. People sit and listen to their boss, just as they listened to their teachers in school—without questioning. If

I ask a Thai co-worker to look into the reason for some problem in the factory process, he will often return with the message that it is hard to say what is causing it. It takes a long time to solve even simple problems, and the lack of imagination revealed is often quite remarkable.

When the light in the overhead projector isn't working, people don't first check to see whether the bulb is broken. Instead they try out different sockets in the room, because there might not be any voltage in the first socket used. Then they wriggle all of the connections a little bit in case there is a break somewhere. If this doesn't work, they go and get a new cable, because one cannot eliminate the possibility of a disconnection somewhere. If all else fails, they go to look for a new bulb as a last resort, and all of a sudden the light is working.

Even though I have been married to a pre-school teacher for many years, it was not until coming to Thailand that I truly realized the importance of stimulating intellectual activity during the formative years—to encourage curiosity and creativity throughout the rest of one's life.

Even though most children in Thailand learn to read and write in school, reading traditions are not well developed here. Reading for pleasure, which is common in the Western world and also in China (and in some neighbouring countries like Burma and Vietnam), does not exist here to any extent, except in the form of comic books, which are quite popular. Historically, most Thai literature was either religious scripture or royal chronicle, which doesn't attract too many people. Contemporary Thai authors are gradually making a name for themselves, but you have to look hard, even in Bangkok bookstores, to find a Thai novel. Reading is simply not a popular leisure activity for Thais. Very seldom do you see a Thai on a train or bus reading a book. I often ask job candidates about their personal interests, and only occasionally do some mention that they like reading. And when asked about what they like to read, the answers are usually computer, fashion, or motor magazines, and cartoons. Literature definitely does not amuse the modern Thai generation. On the other hand, business and management books are much more popular, as they are seen as a short cut to success. Our company utilizes advanced manufacturing processes, but it is difficult to find a textbook dealing with the technology involved. But on many of the bookshelves in the factory, there are scores of bestsellers by American 'business gurus.'

At the international university in Bangkok where I lecture, it is interesting to observe the performance of the different nationalities. In my class there are students from various Asian countries with different educational traditions. In my opinion, these seem to have some connection with their ability to absorb technical knowledge. Almost every year, the Chinese students are among the top achievers, and are often rewarded for outstanding academic performance. It is very likely that the Confucian traditions, which place emphasis on intellectual studies, still prevail in modern China. Without being aware of this cultural heritage, the Chinese students seem to be better equipped for academic studies than their Thai friends. The Chinese interest in reading and learning is also very evident when visiting China itself. In most cities you can easily find bookshops on the main streets, with a great selection of volumes on many different subjects. When travelling, you often see Chinese people reading a book, which is in complete contrast to what you will come across in Thailand.

With the rote system in place, children's imaginations are neutered at a very early age, and that hinders their ability, or desire, to pick up a book full of words and actually picture a scene in their heads. The expression to 'read a book' does not have the same meaning to a Thai as it does to a Westerner. To read a book in Thailand seems to have a negative connotation: it means 'to study'—and this is something you did in school, and thus not a leisure activity.

Gunilla often entertains Khun Yaa's (our neighbour and the football coach [see last chapter]) kids with various activities, and also tries to get them interested in reading children's books. The kids enjoyed this, so she bought some advanced books in Bangkok and gave them to Khun Yaa, suggesting that he read them for his children. He looked at Gunilla with an expression next to horror on his face. Did Gunilla really mean that *he* should read these books to his kids? He pushed the piles of books back across the table to Gunilla and asked her to do the reading for the children. "You are the teacher; you can do the reading." In exchange, he promised to help us with the Thai-language manual for our car.

One morning while having breakfast in a hotel, I was looking at the letters page in one of the English-language dailies. One of the letters was titled, "Thais are happier not to read books." The author made the case that Thai reading habits are closely linked to their social behaviour. Thais enjoy socializing in groups, and reading is not a social activity; instead, it prevents the reader from enjoying a happy social life. Being a passionate reader myself, I did not fully agree with this opinion, but then I raised my eyes from the newspaper and watched the other guests having breakfast. In a corner at the far end of the restaurant,

a serious-looking foreigner was drinking his morning coffee alone, absorbed in a brick-sized international bestseller. In the middle of the room, a big group of Thais was gathered around a table laden with numerous dishes, and their happy voices were clear evidence of their having a good time.

In my position in the company, I'm expected to keep up to date with technical developments related to our business, and I regularly review a number of industry magazines. At first, I distributed copies of articles of interest to the relevant people in order to keep them informed. After some time, I found that most of these copies went unread, and I was asked to make concise reviews of the articles to make it easier for the Thais to understand. I fully appreciate that reading technical and scientific articles in a foreign language is difficult. But with prevailing Thai habits, there is little practice in reading even in Thai. When confronted with a complicated text in a foreign language, this becomes a true obstacle.

16. Safety First

During our time in Thailand, we have observed the construction industry at close quarters. In the beginning, when the mill and company houses were still one big building site, we only had to look through our hotel-room window to get free entertainment. The first thing we noticed about a Thai construction site is that it is swarming with at least as many women as men. As soon as there is a machine involved, however, it is the men who take charge, while the women join up when something has to be carried.

The men dig and hoe by hand, and the soil is transported away in plastic baskets that two women carry between them. The men are wiry and weather-beaten; the women are robust. These female workers definitely do not look like the beautiful, smiling, slender-limbed Thais depicted in advertisements. Their faces are considerably wider and dark-skinned, with coarser features peeping out from under their straw hats. They are more representative of country folk. Many call themselves Lao and say that they are from Isaan, the arid rural tableland of northeast Thailand. They protect themselves from the sun by covering up from top to toe. They wear balaclavas, and on top of that a wide-brimmed straw hat. I find it hard to imagine myself wearing this amount of clothing if I had to dig a ditch in forty-degree heat, but there is a vanity factor at work here: the only protection these women are seeking is against the sun turning their skin any darker. Thais, to put it bluntly, hate dark skin. This is more to do with a kind of class consciousness than racism. In the Thai mindset, only peasants and manual labourers who toil in the sun are 'cursed' with dark skin, and most Thais will do all they can to avoid the sun. On the beaches, you will never ever see a Thai sunbathing.

Workers bring along a big thermos every morning. During the day, they sip at icy cold water—without which, hard work would probably come to a standstill. Women doing heavy manual labour is nothing new in Thailand, where they have always taken a major responsibility in farm work. The traditional farming community is a matriarchal society, where women represent the continuity and security in the family. When the children get married, the son usually moves in with his parents-in-law, while the daughter remains in the household with her husband.

In the past, men were sometimes absent for long periods of time, having either been forced into corvee or military service. Nowadays, rural men—and, more often than not, the whole family—leave for seasonal work at building sites. The women, if left behind, then have to take care of the house and farm. All family members usually return to the village when it gets close to the rice harvesting in December, and during the re-planting of the rice in June. Family bonds are strong, so there are few workers on building sites during these times of the year.

During a project, builders live on or near the site in hastily erected housing: a simple frame of poles and planks, along with some corrugated metal sheets. Whole families with small children live like this for years without access to proper sanitary facilities. I find it hard to understand that it works, but the old-time Swedish navvies who laid out the railroads through the icy wilderness probably lived like this, too. The difference is that on the roofs of these shelters are TV antennas, and in the evenings

people gather around to follow with excitement the game shows and soap operas, of which there appears no limit. The inhabitants of these soaps are the super rich of Bangkok, and the incredible lifestyles depicted are nothing like the rude living conditions of the construction workers. I cannot even imagine what goes through the mind of a dirt-poor, disenfranchised construction labourer as he watches these fantastical TV shows after a hard day's work, at minimum wage, in a muddy or dusty building site.

Workers who do not live on the site are transported to work, packed together like cattle, on a truck. But happy faces peep out from underneath the straw hats and balaclavas. They get a regular salary in cash, which is not impressive but nevertheless affords them the chance of realizing their dreams of a better life.

At the hotel complex alongside the mill, a swimming pool was built at the start of the rainy season. That year, the monsoon was unusually heavy, and the surrounding areas were inundated. Rain does not hinder construction in Thailand, however. A big hole was excavated, first by machine but then by hand, as the workers prepared the concrete moulds with spades and buckets. Throughout this time, the rain kept pouring down. Every morning when the workers looked out from their tin sheds, the hole was half-full with water, and a bucket chain was quickly organized. The hole would be empty by lunchtime and, after the siesta, the workers dug and arranged forms for the concrete foundation. On some days they also managed to fill some parts of the moulds with concrete before the floodgates opened and filled the cavity anew with water. The next morning, it was again time to bring out the bailing buckets. This went on for almost a month before the rains stopped. The swimming pool was eventually finished and ready for Christmas—but not for Christmas as first announced; only Christmas the following year.

Concrete work doesn't always come out perfectly on the first attempt. This isn't a problem, however, since it can always be corrected. One simply chips away at the erroneous bits, or casts some new concrete where needed. It raises some concerns for a foreigner, however, when you see a load-bearing concrete pillar come out of the moulding a bit askew. Especially after seeing the workers manually chipping away a little bit on one side and adding a bit more concrete to the other before the pillar is finally nice and straight. To hack away at concrete by hand is not an easy job, especially when it is done with the most basic tools available. The workers attach a big nail to a rubber-hose handle, and then hit the nail with a stone or maybe a hammer. If enough people are involved, the problem is soon solved. While the women chip away, their children sit down nearby and unconcernedly play together.

Just beside our first temporary offices was another company's headquarters. The firm managed our mill's electrical installations, and their staff was housed in a typical tin shed. Office, storage, and living areas were all under one roof. Each morning, clothes were hung up to dry outside, and chickens pecked around the entrance. The electricians kept a practical array of tools, and when we needed help, we went over to their barracks to borrow what was needed.

One morning, I had to drill some holes in a plank, so I strode over to the shed to get help. Yes, they did have an electric drill; it was simply a matter of finding it. I entered the shed and got an insight into Thai administration on a building site. I could see that finding the drill wasn't going to be easy. In the middle of the floor, a cat was suckling her litter of kittens, and I had to step over her to go further inside. The desk was piled with installation drawings, so the computer that was used for a variety of administrative tasks had been placed on a chair. In a way, this was actually more practical, since you could sit on the floor when using

it. Even though most of the material was on the floor, there was a storage shelf, and that was where we found the drill. The machine didn't work, however, so we had to search for another. A second drill didn't work either. Finally, we did get number three going. It had no plug, but that didn't matter because it worked just as well by sticking the ends of the cable directly into the electrical socket. Sparks flew out of the socket when we finally started to drill a hole.

I was amazed by what could be achieved in Thailand, after witnessing how big industrial projects were completed. Few large buildings in Bangkok have ever collapsed, but maybe that has more to do with the Thais' sensibility in maintaining good relations with the spirits.

At the entrance to most Thai construction sites there is a sign or a banner with "SAFETY FIRST" proudly emblazoned across it to emphasize that the management cares about the welfare of its employees. But when you follow the daily routine of a Thai in the workplace, you witness situations that would make the hair of a Western safety officer turn white overnight. There were serious accidents in our mill, some fatal. Employees have been crushed beneath falling materials, got caught and been drawn inside machines, and fallen from rickety scaffolding. To me, it seemed that people lacked the ability to imagine that an accident could happen at all.

At an early stage, our company set up a safety organization according to an international model, with one central safety committee and several workplace committees. During one meeting, we had been discussing the set-up of a reporting system to follow up on accidents and incidents, but confusion arose about these two concepts. The Western participants cited examples from their earlier industry experience, but still couldn't get across the difference between incident and accident satisfactorily. Finally, a smile of understanding spread over the face of one of the Thais, who described the concepts with an example comprehensible to everyone. If you sit beneath a coconut tree and a coconut falls down on your head, then it is an accident. On the other hand, if the coconut falls without hitting you on the head, it is an incident. After this analogy, there was no longer any misunderstanding.

On the part of management and supervisors, there is a strong belief in the value of safety equipment. All employees, including construction workers, are expected to use protective shoes and hard hats when on the mill premises. But the construction workers, especially, found this

impractical, and these regulations were rarely followed. In spite of disciplinary measures, it was hard to make any significant improvements. Every time there was a serious accident or fatality, the focus on safety equipment was brought to the fore and 'safety officers' were sent out onto the factory floor to find transgressors without safety shoes or hard hats.

The construction workers were meant to use protective shoes, but little effort was made to enforce the rule. Strict enforcement of this regulation would have had the opposite of the intended effect. Quite stable scaffolding is made by tying bamboo canes together in an ingenious fashion. To climb them, however, you need feet like a monkey's. Sometimes it's unnecessary to use scaffolding at all. Barefoot painters climbed, without any safety arrangements, to paint the steel girders. I can casily imagine how disabled a worker wearing protective shoes would feel climbing over such scaffolding, because there are no accompanying wooden gangways as there are with steel scaffold.

Most workers are more willing to wear the protective helmet, and there is even a certain status to be seen in this. Thais love uniforms and being identified as belonging to a certain group: it provides recognition and, on a more mundane level, shows that one has a paid and secure job on an important site. Still, one has to protect oneself against the burning sun when working outdoors in the tropics. The best headgear for this purpose is a wide-brimmed straw hat. How can one combine the need for protection against the sun with the requirement of a protective helmet? That is not a problem for a Thai. He simply places the protective helmet over the straw hat and skillfully balances the two while getting on with his work.

The Thai view on electrical safety has a long way to go before reaching Western standards, and there is usually no requirement of competence to perform electrical installations. There isn't any standardization of electrical sockets or plugs, both American and European connections being found on electrical appliances. The solution in such a situation is to not use any plugs at all, but simply connect the electrical tool by sticking the ends of the wire directly into the socket.

While Johan, a Swedish colleague, was working in Thailand, his family stayed in a Bangkok apartment. When he got a washing machine for their apartment, he made the shop agree to perform the installation. Johan emphasized the importance of the washing machine being installed with protective earth connection, and the shopkeeper asserted that this was not a problem, since they had electricians to perform this. The washing machine was delivered and Johan pointed out the spot on the balcony where the machine was to be fitted. He then left the electrician to work on his own. Eventually the man announced that the job was done according to the directions, and Johan went out on the balcony to inspect the work. The green earth wire was indeed connected, but since it was hard to find any proper earth connection, the electrician had come up with a practical solution: he simply drilled a hole in the tiled floor of the balcony and squeezed in a plastic plug. The earthing-wire was then attached to the plastic plug with a screw. That was as close as one could get to earth on a balcony in Bangkok.

The joining of electrical wires is done in the simplest way possible, seemingly without any apprehensions. One twines the ends together and wraps insulating tape around the join. I got to see quite a range of such solutions for the provision of electricity to the different sites. Welding had to be performed in numerous places, and welding cables from the transformers were laid out across the muddy fields around the mill. Sometimes the cables weren't long enough, so the welders spliced cables together to get the desired length. They would then tie a piece of cloth as insulation around the splice and continue to weld.

One rainy day, I passed one such place where some welding was going on. Two electrical cables on a welding torch had been joined together, with cloth acting as the insulator. The cable was lying in the mud and, as I passed by, there was a spark from the join. The heat made the cloth smoulder. The cloth caught fire and I tried to draw the welder's attention to what had happened. He looked at me in surprise, and then at the

burning cloth. He shrugged his shoulders while I pointed indignantly at the cloth on fire. At last he approached the cloth and stepped on it with his flip-flops, so that the cable disappeared in the mud and the fire was extinguished. He could thereafter continue his welding without the neurotic foreigner having anything to worry about.

17. You May Get A Headache

Administration is quickly introduced into business in developing countries, and Thailand is no exception. When a business grows and the owner can no longer supervise everything personally, he feels a need for increased control. In Thai companies with Chinese traditions, there is such a demand for control over employees' lives that a foreigner can feel insulted. I have never come across so many forms that have to be filled out so many times as during my time working in a Thai company. No wonder so many people in Thailand are occupied with bureaucratic tasks, considering all the bits of paper that have to be reported to a higher authority. All these, in theory, allow the company to be managed in minute detail. But, in reality, they don't seem to be enough to keep the business in order.

The extensive machinery in our mill demanded strict maintenance routines, and worn-out parts, sooner or later, needed to be replaced with spares. Easy access to spare parts is essential in a modern factory. This was not the view of the management. The machines were new, weren't they? And should give many years of trouble-free operation? To keep spare parts, just in case, was an expensive exercise by their way of thinking. When the obstinate foreigners still insisted on spare parts, the philosophy of Thai administration became clear.

The company had been in business for many years and had tried to keep important spare parts in stock. They had, however, given up on this idea, since nobody could ever find the parts when they were finally needed. It was much better to send someone to Bangkok to buy the part when a machine broke down. In the end, this was quicker than trying to find the spare part somewhere in the factory. Confronted with such logic, the foreigner throws up his hands.

My Thai assistant is a very ambitious and orderly woman who keeps a number of ledgers. On one occasion I asked her what kind of book-keeping she was doing at that particular time. She was accounting for the department's office supplies, where the usage of paper clips, pencils, and other things was carefully noted and divided into time periods so that they could be tracked month by month. I wondered in what way this information could be used—and received a surprised look in return. These particulars were necessary, I was told, to plan the orders for our section from the department assigned to administrate the whole company. Office supplies had to be ordered well ahead of time to enable this department to assemble them. The whole order would then go to the purchase department which, in turn, would invite tenders from a couple of suppliers. If we couldn't predict our need for paper clips, we might one day find ourselves without any left! It could take months before we got another delivery.

It is important to control costs in an industrial business, and all the departments did their best not to burden the company with unnecessary expenses. Saving money is a virtue in a Chinese-influenced company, and if people can successfully cut costs, they might get a bonus. The administration department found such a way to cut costs. They simply halved all orders for office supplies. This made everyone aware that they couldn't waste, for instance, paper clips. People discovered that they only received five folders when they had ordered ten, with a note to the effect that the admin department hadn't received any more with the delivery. The various sections simply began ordering double whatever they needed. The office department could nevertheless show that they had made considerable savings.

Early on, I encountered the stamp ordering form. I had given an official letter to our secretary to send out. It turned out not to be so simple. She tilted her head and asked suspiciously if it was really necessary to send the letter by post. Wouldn't it be simpler to fax it? But it was a bit hard to send paper samples by fax, so the secretary then brought out the stamp order form and asked me to fill it out. A fair amount of detail had to be provided, such as the intended recipient, the purpose of the package, reassurance that it was an official letter, and more. Then it had to be signed by the authorized person and sent to the accounting department so they could allocate cash for the purchase of stamps. On the following day, the normal delivery car went to the post office to buy stamps and stamp my letter. In spite of all these regulations, the letter never reached its destination.

It is at times like this that the most patient foreigner might despair at the level of bureaucracy in Thailand. Our secretary, holding a degree in industrial psychology, had a fine-tuned ability to read a tormented foreigner's thoughts. She empathized with me once with a comforting word that was of great help in many stressful situations and came to be something of a mantra: "Mr. Kolmodin, sometimes you just have to accept things, otherwise you can get a headache."

It is quite an experience to visit a post office in the Thai countryside. Even in smaller towns, the bank is usually an opulent modern creation in glass and concrete that towers above other buildings. In Thailand, the god Mammon usurps all others, just like everywhere else. But the post office blends in, low-rise and covered in dust. When you enter a bank, you are met with a cool, air-conditioned environment and staff wearing neat office attire. All transactions are done through computer terminals, and you feel far removed from the chaotic trading on the pavements outside. The customers line up in neat queues between chrome-plated posts in front of the counters, and a policeman is seated discreetly in a corner with his automatic rifle on his knees. If you have special business, you get to sit down in an armchair and the bank manager might even help you to fill out the form in Thai.

But in the post office you step back at least three decades. There is no air conditioning here; window shutters are left open to allow a draught, and big ceiling fans stir the air just a little. Behind the worn counter, clerks wear khaki-coloured government uniforms decorated with epaulettes and more and more badges of rank. Customers cluster before the counter. No queue here: you have to thrust yourself forward into an opening. You've got to be alert, otherwise someone further back with long arms will get in first. When someone else does push in front, you have to restrain your Western sense of order. If you do object, all you'll receive is a big Thai smile in return.

Buying stamps is normally not a very complicated errand at the post office, but when a foreigner comes in and asks for twenty stamps for letters to be sent to Europe, the situation for the clerk becomes alarming.

"How much does each letter weigh? Less than twenty grams? That will be 24 baht."

"In that case, can I buy twenty 24-baht stamps?"

"No, we don't have any 24-baht stamps."

"What kind of stamps do you have?"

"We have 6-baht stamps."

"Well, can I then buy eighty 6-baht stamps?"

"No, that is not possible, I don't have that many. Hang on a second!"

In the best case scenario, the postmaster is seated behind a big empty desk set further back, and the clerk may borrow a big bunch of keys to open the safe and sign out a sheet of stamps. On one occasion, the postmaster had gone for lunch and taken the keys with him. When we returned later that afternoon, he still hadn't come back, and so we had to leave the post office empty-handed that day.

In the cities and bigger towns, computers are only just making their entrance into the post office system. Upcountry, handwritten records are still kept. The whole system consists of small forms with sheets of carbon paper in between, or forms that have to be separated and glued to the appropriate package. The forms need to be stamped as well, and this is done with an authority that is heard throughout the room. It takes a certain skill to manage all these slips in the draught from the big ceiling fans, and the clerk has a system with a number of weights and clips to keep receipts and dispatch notes in their place on the counter. Sometimes I wonder whether it is really possible to keep track of all these transactions with this system, and suspect that a lot of letters and packages don't reach their destination.

Once, I wanted to send a big envelope with my income tax return form to Sweden. Nobody escapes the Swedish tax authority, not even by hiding out in the Thai countryside. I asked for the letter to be sent as 'Registered.' That would cost me 150 baht. There weren't that many stamps in the till, so the clerk would stick them on later. Receipts were written, stamped, glued on, and I paid my 150 baht—but that envelope never reached its destination either. After all, why would the postal clerk be interested in a crazy Swede's annual tax forms! I wonder where the money went and where the letter ended up. In spite of this kind of trouble, the post office is always a more exciting place to visit than the bank.

18. Business Life

Many companies in Thailand are under the strict control of a family clan and a group of close colleagues and associates. This originates from the business traditions in ancient China, where merchants were harassed and sometimes banished by the emperor. The emperor's spies were everywhere, and only close family members could be trusted. Families that migrated to other countries found themselves in a foreign environment that did not always greet immigrants with open arms. The Chinese were different: aside from the language, they didn't look like the Thais, and they dressed differently. When the Chinese settled down in Thai rural society, they brought with them their business traditions, and soon dominated trading in the countryside. Thai farmers eventually felt tricked when they found themselves depending on the Chinese when they needed to borrow money for grain. The Chinese probably experienced a certain chilly atmosphere in return, and thus closed ranks to protect their interests.

In old China, businessmen had to endure many hardships. When the emperor's power eventually declined and trading developed more freely, new rulers appeared on the scene. The European colonial powers aggressively and brutally pursued their own interests in the 1800s, and secured profitable trade deals. They resorted to force of arms to control lucrative markets such as opium distribution inside China. European trading stations and colonies were established on Chinese territory. Chinese traders regarded the European invasion with great disapproval, since the Europeans were driven by no more than the laws of Mammon. One could never trust a European, and the Chinese wouldn't let any 'long nose' inside their business.

With the experience of generations of hardship and deprivation at the hands of malicious foreigners and badgering imperial officers, the Chinese businessman of today only feels safe surrounded by his close

family. The head of the family maintains a very strong position, and the rest of the family is both indebted to and dependent upon him. It is the patriarch who holds the key to the strong box, and no major transactions are allowed without his approval.

In one English-language newspaper, I read about a young man who gave a less than flattering description of his Chinese father. The father wasn't good-looking, nor did he behave decently in front of others. But the modern young man didn't mind this, because it was what the old man had in his wallet that mattered, since his father was paying for his studies. The old Confucian teachings about the hierarchical order of society and the moral concepts of diligence and humility towards authority also play a role in the respect for the family head.

Within the clan there is also an obvious hierarchy. The oldest child doesn't have to worry about being questioned by younger siblings. All of the children usually work within the family company to help with those duties the patriarch deems essential. Offspring who want to go their own way will no longer have any input into the family business. This kind of central control was effective in a Chinese general store, but is an anachronism in the modern business world, especially in international banks and industrial conglomerates. Nevertheless, it is still common in Thailand for family members to hold most of the important positions in such concerns. These positions can only be entrusted to people one can rely on. Only from the nearest family members can one expect total loyalty. Outsiders are viewed with distrust and have to be kept under careful scrutiny to prevent them from embezzling or squandering the company's assets.

To a foreigner working in such an organization, the atmosphere can occasionally feel insulting, when his ability to make decisions is close to non-existent. The foreigner may put forward suggestions which then have to be submitted to the judgement of the family. It doesn't matter if the Westerner has special qualifications and was recruited because of his knowledge. All major decisions have to be made by the patriarch or his close associates, even if they lack competence. It is more important that the decision maker is loyal to the company than having expertise in the area he is supposed to manage. The prevailing attitude is still that a 'long nose' cannot be loyal and cannot be trusted with making decisions.

In larger companies, it can prove difficult to find family members for all the senior positions, but that can be solved by offering these posts to close friends of the family or to friends that are in some way indebted to the family. When Thais have difficulties in financing their higher education, they often have to find some kind of scholarship, or a sponsor to pay for their studies. Companies might provide the necessary funding, but will demand that the student pledge to work for the company for some period of time, or to pay back tuition costs directly. When a student completes his education, there is usually a position awaiting him, even though he may not be ready for the task or doesn't have the adequate competence. He may end up in an inappropriate position, but the company has at least managed to place a loyal person there. The company is also keen to take advantage of its investment and does not willingly let the student go. This means, in reality, that the student will be tied to an employer for an unforeseeable period of time.

In larger companies, the CEO cannot personally keep up with all activities on a daily basis, but the interest in attending to details is still noticeable. In accordance with Chinese business traditions, detailed figures and accounts must be reported to the highest level. The foreigner usually views this accounting as an obsession with figures, and it is uncertain whether management can really interpret and make use of such information. The boss, however, gets a certain feeling of security at having all this information to hand, and employees become aware that their work is monitored and reported to the boss.

A foreigner needs to adapt to be able to function within a Thai company. Many Westerners have a lot of technical and management experience, and it is for this reason they have been invited to work in Thailand. At the same time, Westerners have to accept that working with Thais is not the same as working with Westerners. If not, they'll find it frustrating when things don't get done properly.

Thai views on working life are different from those in the West. One important requisite for the Thai workday is the concept of *sanuk*, which roughly translates as 'fun.' Those who work in the new industrial companies are mostly young. In our company, the average age of employees is below thirty, and most are highly social. They don't screen off individual work spaces in the office. Instead they put their desks close together so they can have contact with their workmates.

When the mill was starting up, the workload on my laboratory staff wasn't too heavy. However, when production turned into full swing, they were fully occupied. Some complained and said that they no longer had time to take a break and maintain their social life. They were surprised when I told them they could no longer take a nap during work.

To have *sanuk* also reflects another view of work that has disappeared from Western society. In Thailand, there is no clear divide between work and spare time. Work is an integral part of life, and you spend a good part of it at the workplace. When knock-off time arrives, there is little rush to get home. Employees might stay behind to chat with their colleagues or to read the paper. The air-conditioned workplace might very well be nicer than the living conditions at home. If I am working late, I sometimes go for a walk around the premises before leaving. Often there will be people staying behind, and I almost have to force them to go home.

One day, I was going on a company tour with some colleagues to one of our raw material suppliers. Interest in the tour was high, as it is nice to get out from the office. Departure was scheduled for 11:00 a.m. and I hurried to be on time. I was a few minutes late, but I was still the first person at the meeting point, except for the bus driver. After a few phone calls, I managed to round up the whole group and herd them onto the bus, and we left only half an hour late. We arrived after a good two-hour trip. First we had lunch with some of the suppliers at a hotel down by the sea. In accordance with Thai tradition, many delicious dishes were crowded on the table. By the time lunch was over, it was 4:00 p.m. and maybe time to go to the factory.

When we finally arrived at the factory outside the city of Rayong, the marketing manager gave us a very interesting presentation that went on for an hour. After that, we were served some refreshments. Time passed quickly, but nobody, bar me, looked at their watch. Everyone was having such a great time. Then it was time for a guided tour. When the tour was over, it was 7:00 p.m. and, after the appropriate pleasantries were exchanged, it was finally time to go home. Or so I thought. But by this stage my colleagues had become hungry again. A Thai eats happily and often, and so now we had to find a restaurant—fortunately not a difficult task in Thailand. Once again, we sat around a table laden with little dishes and rice bowls. It looked like it was going to be a long night, so I had a pint of beer to help me sleep on the bus—if, in fact, we ever got back on the bus again.

We finally did, sated and content, but we left the restaurant in what I thought was the wrong direction. Of course, my companions now wanted to go to the night market in Rayong. There were many exciting things to see and buy. Dried and salted squid, jellyfish, rays, and shrimps sat on the stalls. My colleagues bought these delicacies to take home. After all, it's nice to chew on a dried squid when you are sitting at your desk.

It was midnight when we finally got to the mill. There was still talk of karaoke, but everyone ended up heading home instead. I was greeted by a worried Gunilla, but I'd had a nice day in spite of the late hour.

And that, in Thailand, is *sanuk*!

Leisure pastimes and hobbies do not play as important a role in a Thai's life as they do in a foreigner's. When the Western specialists arrived at our company, they tried to get to know their Thai colleagues. Victor, responsible for one of the production departments, invited his new friends to a dinner one night so they could all get to know each other better. At the dinner, Victor talked about his passion for sailing in the Swedish archipelago. On asking his Thai guests about their leisure activities, there was an awkward silence and they looked at each other, embarrassed. Victor had to rescue the situation quickly and return to the main theme of the evening—namely eating together.

Most working Thai people are entitled to only one week of vacation a year. This doesn't sound like much to a foreigner, but many Thais don't really know what to do with time off. In December, when I asked my assistant whether the department's staff had any outstanding holidays owed to them, I got the reply that most of them had a few. I asked how to schedule our department's work up until the end of the year in order to manage a scenario if all the employees took holidays at the same time. "No problem." I was informed that no one needed any year-end holiday, even though remaining holidays that employees hadn't used would be null and void. But they did get a new holiday allocation for the next year, so what was the problem?

Going on holiday—especially to a foreign country— is a strange concept in Thailand even though, ironically, many Thai people earn their living from the constant stream of foreigners on vacation. Often, instead of going to a beach or the mountains, one helps a relative who is in need of an extra pair of hands. A Thai business acquaintance once wondered what I had been doing during my four-week holiday in Sweden. He told me that during his ten-year career, he had never taken a holiday with his family. Either the children had been so young that it had been too cumbersome to travel, or his wife had been so occupied with her work that they couldn't arrange a joint vacation.

There are, however, a great number of public holidays in Thailand, usually commemorating a royal or religious occasion. Most of these are single-day holidays scattered throughout the calendar, and Thais are obliged to take them as part of their annual leave allowance to make up for the few days they are allowed from their employer. Roads and resorts thus become congested as the whole country takes off on short breaks at the same time, with many people taking an extra Friday or Monday as a day off to extend a long weekend.

The relationship between Thai managers and their co-workers is different from the West. A boss is expected to look after his subordinate's interests and show social responsibility for his staff. I have never been visited by so many weeping girls who want to vent their anxieties, but this confiding relationship is not achieved immediately. You have to gain their trust by how you act.

A Thai manager is expected to take his staff out for dinner at least a couple of times a year. It is always the boss who pays the bill. Early on, I took my staff to a New Year's party and, with the help of my assistant, we had a lovely Thai dinner. The boys and girls, in their mid-twenties, probably felt a little shy when they seated themselves around the table. When I asked them what they wanted to drink, most confined themselves to water, while only a few brave ones ordered Coke. I ordered a beer and asked one lad, whom I knew liked drinking, to join me. He jumped at the chance and, after that, one after the other ordered beer and we all toasted each other. By the end of the evening, everyone was drinking beer. I had a bit of a bad conscience for having enticed innocent young Thais with the lure of alcohol.

By gaining the trust of his staff, the manager at the same time gets a very loyal workforce who are willing to put up with extra duties whenever needed. This sounds like an ideal relationship to have in the workplace. However, there is a downside. The boss is expected to look after his employees. The subordinates, in turn, protect their boss by not reporting unpleasant incidents.

Robert, another production manager, never really managed to gain his staff's loyalty and couldn't get some tasks done. When maintenance work was required and the operators weren't busy with supervising the machinery, Robert tried to get them to clean underneath and around the machines. This was a hot and strenuous task. As soon as Robert showed the foreman what he wanted done, the other employees disappeared as if by magic. The foreman couldn't find them until the time for maintenance was over and production was to be resumed. Obviously the operators were hiding, with the foreman's consent, to avoid having to do the dirty work.

If a Thai has made his way up the ladder of society, by education or a job that doesn't require manual labour, it is seen as reaping the benefits of good deeds done in a previous life. Buddhist promises about freedom from mundane sufferings have an obvious down-to-earth interpretation: fortune, beauty, power—and freedom from manual labour. If you have reached a certain position, you are entitled to these rewards.

For some Thai men, maintaining a single long fingernail is a traditional way of warding off evil spirits who may wish to deprive them of their manhood. But this also has another advantageous consequence, as it is a way to show people that one has climbed the social ladder and no longer has to carry out heavy labour. When the young machine operators arrived at the company for training, many came directly from technical school. They had, by virtue of their education, grown their nails very long. They soon discovered that working in a process industry is not an office job, and that their long, beautiful nails were a danger. Some operators initially used their nails as an excuse not to do maintenance work. They realized however, one by one, that they would have to sacrifice their nails to do their job properly.

The company has a fleet of pick-up trucks. Some of the drivers see their position as an important step upwards, and indicate this by keeping an exquisitely long nail. They handle the steering wheel and the gear stick with style, but that's about it. When we were finally due to leave our temporary offices in the barracks and move to the new accomodation, I ordered a pick-up truck to load our belongings. The driver stopped the

truck in front of the building and then stretched out to sleep in his seat while the truck bed was loaded. We had to wake him up when the truck was full. He quickly and efficiently drove to the new office, and promptly fell asleep again once the truck stopped. It was pointless to ask him to help unload the truck—he would have broken his nail.

Our company uniforms made us look very anonymous, even though our names were embroidered on the jacket. There was no way to indicate one's position. But a vain person usually finds a solution. One manager smartened up his uniform by exchanging the ordinary grey buttons for gold ones. The irreverent Europeans soon nicknamed him 'The General.'

But you shouldn't really laugh at people's desire to display their position in the hierarchy. To a Thai, this is very important. With higher position comes status, and even power. I spent long hours with my co-workers discussing the organization of our department. They did not want a flat management structure. It was more a question of how many levels of authority that one wanted to create, because such an organization offers possibilities for promotion. The lure of promotion prompts employees into excelling at their work, and this can only make a positive contribution to the company.

19. Doing Business

From early childhood, a Thai learns to manage money. Even the youngest pre-school child arrives at class with a coin scrunched up in the hem of his school uniform and fastened with a rubber band. After lunch, the children gather around a candy stall to buy sweets with their coins. Heavy bargaining ensues. Children also help out with their parents' business, and they get used to dealing with the customers at the market stall or noodle shop. They soon become good at counting and giving correct change. An early awareness of money is instilled in the children, and this remains throughout their lives.

Businesspeople are the dominant force in Thai society today, taking over the role from the military and civil service of yesteryear. A business can be something as small as a stall at a local market, where the nightly catch of grasshoppers is grilled and sold, or as big as the conglomerates that conduct international trade in rice and oil. There is definitely no lack of initiative within the Thai business world, and immense individual fortunes are created through trade. During the last couple of years, real estate has been a most lucrative area, but after the 1997 Asian financial crisis, the land market collapsed like a house of cards and many people were ruined.

People may start a business with very modest resources. Through industrious work and the whole family pitching in, the business can, from modest beginnings, become huge. Our industrial park acted like a magnet, attracting all kinds of merchants. At the end of the country road, one man put up a tin shack for a drum of petrol and a small pump. He attracted customers away from the Shell station a few kilometres away by offering discount rates. The whole family helped, and it was often the children who were responsible for filling up the cars. The elder sister sat in the shade, keeping track of the till in a plastic lunchbox, while her small brothers and sisters got to operate the pump. One year later, the man exchanged his drum for a proper fuel tank, and the hand-pump for

a second-hand electric pump. One year after that, he built a real petrol station in concrete with a roof over the petrol pumps, and erected a big illuminated billboard.

In the Thai business world, there is no real concept of set working hours. As long as they can earn money, traders keep their places open. If, in the middle of the night, you have to fill up your car, you might drive into a closed petrol station, honk your horn, and get a tank full of petrol as soon as someone gets out of bed. This happened to us one night, and we didn't have to wait long at all. The attendant was asleep on a camp bed next to the pump. He just had to stand up and lift the nozzle before flopping back into bed again.

Behind the new petrol station, I caught sight of another 'new' tin shed. On a pole attached to the roof, a used tyre was hanging, and a hand-painted sign read: "Tyre Service, 24 Hours A Day." Two industrious young men had started a new business, living with their wives in a simple hut. On the ground in front of the shed, they fixed punctures on both motorbikes and trucks. If you needed help with a flat, you only had to knock on the shed, and soon your tyre would be fixed. Neither did they charge extra for fixing tyres outside 'normal' working hours.

Having Saturdays and Sundays free for yourself, which most Westerners take for granted, is simply not the case in Thailand. Public institutions—schools, post offices, government offices, banks—have fallen for the Western indulgence of shutting down at the weekends. For the rest of the business community, however, there is no clear distinction made between Saturday, Sunday, and a normal working day. Shops are open and, in the market, trading goes on at full bore. Even people working for a modern industrial company cannot always be guaranteed a free Sunday. The boss might want a meeting and, since the employees are usually free of their normal duties on Sunday, what better time to have it? A Thai doesn't believe this type of request is unreasonable.

A Westerner might feel that Thai people's intense interest in costs and prices is rude, but to them it is totally natural to ask you how much you paid for your new clothes, your wife's necklace, or your fancy hotel last weekend. The exchange rate is followed with much interest, as is the economic situation for the entire country. Many families still live in a traditional agricultural setting, where the size of the harvest and the price of rice, sugar, and tapioca are of vital importance.

No foreigner who visits Thailand can avoid the very flexible pricing of goods offered in shops and markets. You have to devote some time to bargaining for both parties to agree on a reasonable price. As a foreigner, you have to be prepared for the initial offer to be twice as high as the Thai price. If you can speak a little bit of Thai, and take the time, you can quite easily lower the price to a more reasonable level. After some practice, your bargaining skills are rewarded as you pick up on Thai bargaining methods. The main rule, however, is to take the time. Gunilla could spend half the afternoon at the local market-place shopping for dinner. She enjoys it and always seems to get the best prices.

A shopping trip to a local market can turn out to be really exciting. Besides the haggling over the price, there is also the uncertainty of finding what one is after. Some shops in a small Thai town resemble the old-fashioned general stores that I remember from my childhood in Sweden. If you look long enough, almost everything can be found—from nail clippers to fishing nets. There are also modern and more specialized shops but, even in these places, the range of merchandise can be surprising. In the village, there is a shop that mainly sells kitchen utensils. This being the countryside, you can also buy other kitchen essentials: gas bottles, stoves, pesticides, rat poison, and different types of rice stored in large sacks. It is a shop for the person who wants to completely furnish a new kitchen country style.

Sometimes you cannot find a shop that has the item you are after—but, sooner or later, it always works out. Gunilla had to buy paraffin for a lamp, so we could have some light during a power cut. She went to the nearest town and thought it best to start her inquiries at a petrol station. It wasn't that easy to describe what she wanted to buy, so she got hold of a pen and drew a paraffin lamp. The owner beckoned her daughter over and there was a short conversation, after which the girl took her bike and disappeared down the street. After a few minutes, she returned and handed Gunilla a length of wick for the lamp. That was almost right, and Gunilla continued her description of paraffin. A new discussion arose, and the daughter disappeared again on her bike. This time she came back and handed over some paraffin in a plastic bag. Gunilla took the opportunity to ask about pins, the next item on her shopping list. The girl jumped on her bike again. In this way, Gunilla was able to acquire all the items on her list. This goes to show that, in Thailand, with some patience and improvization, you can get almost anything you want.

As we have seen, business is today a Chinese speciality that has been practically instilled into the Chinese—and Thai—genes. Most trading companies and banks in Thailand are controlled by Chinese families. The type of business doesn't matter. It can be anything from lending out money to Thai farmers who need to borrow for rice seed for the next season's crop, to transferring funds from dubious institutions to speculate on the property market in Bangkok or Singapore.

Many Thai people harbour the dream of one day opening their own business. In our company, most of my young co-workers have some formal engineering education. Once in a while, I ask them about their dreams for the future, and they tell me that they are saving money to start their own businesses. It is trading that attracts the interest of the Thais, even engineers and technicians, not manufacturing or science. Those that don't plan to start their own company strive to win a scholarship to the United States to study business administration. In Thailand, 'MBA' is the new mantra.

This interest in trading is noticeable even in a manufacturing company. The Thais view sales as the most important aspect of business, with the manufacturing department sometimes considered a costly appendage. The marketing and purchasing departments are the heart and soul of the business, where all the deals are made. The control of these functions is very important, and is only entrusted to the most reliable employees.

When it comes to business on a higher level, negotiations in price and payments are a complicated art form. A foreigner is usually accustomed to calling on the purchasing department to requisition any necessary items. It is not that simple in a Thai company characterized by Chinese trading traditions, where people seem to have limitless time. If it is possible to negotiate a more advantageous deal by prolonging the negotiations, there don't seem to be any time constraints.

Thai companies often have a very narrow economic view. As a Westerner, one has to be aware that there is a personal aspect, even in big business. Control over the purchasing department is highly sought after because of the possibility of getting money on the side of any deal that the company negotiates. The choice of a supplier is not restricted solely to what is best for the company, but is also based on what's good for the head of the purchasing department—a couple of percent of the entire order can wind up in his hands. A senior member of our company was involved in a multi-billion-baht contract, and he pushed the limits of what is considered acceptable, even in a Thai company. He was transferred to a peripheral position and had to live with the nickname 'Ten Percent.'

Contracts have to be written with care in order to open up opportunities for discounts or late payments. A natural part of the business process is to provide clauses in the contract so that, later, the customer can argue that the supplier has not fully fulfilled his obligations. I was asked by our marketing department to prepare product specifications, and compiled what I thought was the most relevant information for our customers. The manager of the sales department told me that the information would have to be much more detailed and include tolerance ranges. When I explained that the customer had little use for these kind of specifications, I was told that the customer's purchasing department needed this information because, otherwise, they would not be able to find any faults with the product and, accordingly, get special discounts.

Purchasing raw materials at favourable prices is extremely important, of course. Even for smaller purchases, it is preferable to get three tenders. Then, negotiations with the potential suppliers take place to get an even more favourable deal. The quality of the goods is not really an issue at this stage, the price being the determining factor for what is finally purchased. And to arrive at the lowest price for the deal, time is not important. Delivery times often don't matter, so, if the purchasing department can get a better price, they will do so, even to the detriment of other departments. During the construction of the mill, the workers ran out of gravel for the concrete while the purchasing department was re-negotiating the price with the gravel supplier. The goal of the purchasing department was solely to keep the cost of materials low, and they took no responsibility for the delays that their misguided thriftiness had caused.

In our company, we use various chemicals in the manufacturing process, and on one occasion the purchasing department informed us that they had found a new supplier who could deliver at considerably lower prices. This sounded good to begin with, but it turned out that the new product had a lower percentage by weight of the chemical we required. In the end, it turned out that it was more expensive to use the new supplier. This narrow economic view on costs is not limited to the purchasing department, but extends into the manufacturing sector as well.

In Thailand, people prefer to work on cutting costs that are easy to spot, but they find it harder to view the business as a whole. It is much easier to create an understanding of reduced costs than for absent revenue, which is a much more abstract concept. This kind of thinking is quite frustrating for a Western industrialist who has been taught concepts such as efficiency improvement and reducing losses as a way to increase the company's profit margin. The purchasing department does their best to reduce company expenditures by not buying unnecessary spare parts, but when an entire production line is halted for several hours, or even a whole day, because a fuse worth a couple of dollars is not immediately available in stock, a Western production manager becomes exasperated.

In my previous working life in Sweden, manpower in the company was always an important issue, and labour costs were always under scrutiny in order to maintain acceptable profitability. In bad times it was always staff levels at the top of the agenda for review. Many investments were justified by the potential for reducing manpower. Even though companies announce with pride that their staff is their most valuable asset, it is the employees who suffer when cost reduction is to be executed.

When I first arrived in Thailand, I was impressed by the administration building of the company, and assumed that it must be a very big enterprise, with all the staff working at their small desks lined up in rows. Office girls dressed in neat uniforms and surrounded by piles of paper were busy with their computers. I later realized that the number of office staff is a poor indicator of the size of a Thai company, but rather reflects the complexity of the organization. A big office makes an impression on visitors and, to some extent, demonstrates the power of the company. The same desire for a show of power can be seen in the high-rise bank 'palaces' in Bangkok.

Labour costs do not have the same significance in the cost structure of a manufacturing company in Thailand as they do in Europe or North America, and this is of course the reason why so many international companies establish factories with labour-intensive production in Thailand. When investments are considered in Thai companies, the possibility of replacing automated equipment with additional manpower is often considered. Capital is limited and expensive, whereas labour is cheap and abundant. In the industrial park next to the mill, there are a number of manufacturing companies that employ thousands of mainly young women in assembling electronics or in textile production. But even with the modest wages offered to the Thais, the profit margins for these companies are narrow, and even cheaper labourers from neighbouring countries are shipped in to compete with the Thais for jobs. The number of employees is seldom a topic for discussion. On the contrary, some companies are proud of creating such job 'opportunities' and see a large workforce as a contribution to society.

Pulp and paper manufacturing is a capital-intensive industry and its success is, to a large extent, governed by the economy of scale. With bigger machinery, productivity increases and the labour cost per produc-

tion unit is reduced. For a Thai company competing in the international market, it is still possible to be generous when it comes to the number of people occupied in production. Our company has almost twice as many employees as a similar paper-mill in Western Europe.

When we were considering an expansion of the production capacity for A4 copy-paper and the installation of a second sheeting line, the design of the machinery was carefully reviewed. How could the investment costs be reduced? The final step in the production line, where the paper packages were put in boxes and stacked on pallets, could be done manually instead of the expensive automated equipment suggested by the machine supplier. Along with the machine installation, the recruitment and training of a large number of staff was arranged for the manual part of the new production line. When production started, the staff had to adapt to the continuous stream of packages on the conveyor belt. It was a true team effort, but when the speed of the machine was increased, it became more and more difficult for the team to keep up. Even with additional staff working at the end of the line, the final packing process became a bottleneck, and the originally proposed automated equipment for boxing and palletizing was reviewed again.

◈

Commercial interests in Thailand have a strong influence over the development of society. Other interests hold less sway. Among younger Thais, there is an increasing interest in protecting the environment and taking a role in conservation issues. It is, however, an uneven battle between commercial and conservation interests. Large tracts of land have been set aside as conservation areas in Thailand, but, as we have seen, it is impossible to protect them from illegal logging, poaching, and tourism exploitation. The Thai view on national parks also contributes to commercial exploitation. To many Thais, a national park is not a sanctuary for widlife, but a recreation area with restaurants and hotels. In their wake, souvenir sellers, karaoke bars, and massage parlours quickly spring up. Areas that ten years ago were pristine have quickly been transformed into tourist traps with loud and garish entertainment.

Even where forests are 'protected' they are continually abused. Resort operators infringe upon such areas; logging continues; the wealthy put up huge mansions and villas; and motor rallies are held—with scores of noisy, smoke-belching sports vehicles tearing through the jungle—as a supposed means of helping to protect the forest and the birds and animals that live there! On the 'paradise' beaches, you can no longer hear the waves rolling ashore for the disco music. Moonlight has to compete with the flashing lanterns that hang between the palm trees and adorn the beer stalls set back off the sand.

As long as representatives from the commercial sector fill the government and influential positions in society, conservationists will find it hard to make their voices heard. Unfortunately, this short-sightedness leads to the exploitation of Nature. Tourism quickly leads to littering, with garbage dumps spoiling scenic attractions. This forces tourists to search for less exploited areas. There are still gems of untouched Nature that you can find off the beaten track, but they become fewer and fewer each year.

20. **Between People**

Westerners in Thailand often find the business climate much tougher than what they are used to at home. To some extent, this is due to lax legislation that can favour the more powerful parties at the expense of the weaker. Business between people of different nationalities is also affected by their cultural beliefs, and each party's perception of the other. The concept of 'love your neighbour as yourself' is not held by Thais unless it can benefit the individual. They willingly do favours, but look upon these deeds as investments that will hopefully return dividends in the not-too-distant future. They see to their own interests and have to protect them against the surrounding world.

The honest foreigner usually has an open attitude in business, perhaps even a naïve one. He wants to come to an agreement that is of advantage to both parties. The Thai businessman will have a different view. He looks upon the foreigner with some suspicion, and the old stories about the long-noses during colonial times probably still have a significant impact on Sino-Thai businessmen. It seems that many business agreements in Thailand are negotiated on the basis that your counterpart is probably trying to trick you and, therefore, you should trick him as much as you can in return.

When a deal has been made and the contract is signed by both parties, Westerners expect both parties to stick to it. This is not always the case in Thailand. New circumstances can arise that the Thai businessman feels justify him in breaking the contract. He might blame general economic difficulties. This excuse was used by many companies in Southeast Asia during the financial crisis of 1997, even though there may not have been an urgent crisis for any of them. Employees in a lot of these companies had their salaries reduced by up to thirty percent during this period, with the promise of repayment in better times, when the economy picked up. These 'better times' are defined by the company, and employees might only get re-paid if still in the employ of the same company. As an employee in a Thai firm, the concept of legislative rights is a nebulous one, and the right to interpret any employment contract is in the hands of the employer.

It is difficult for unions to gain a foothold in Thai companies, as all employers look upon unions as troublemakers. During the 1970s, with civil wars in neighbouring countries and a communist insurgency within Thailand's borders, unions were villified as communist stooges and simply forbidden. Today's company managers might have a more reasonable view, but see no need to allow unions into their workforce. Unions arrange demonstrations when salaries are cut, or when a promised bonus fails to materialize. Sometimes they even set the factory alight in protest. Fire insurance doesn't cover arson and, as a company manager, one cannot afford to permit a union which would do such things.

International trade agreements sometimes include a committment to adhere to ILO (International Labour Organization) conventions, which do not make any exceptions for local conditions in countries like Thailand. Sourcing of raw material for the pulp and paper industry has been under scrutiny from environmental organizations aiming to control logging in natural forests. International forestry certification schedules have been established for ensuring that logging is carried out with environmental, social, and economic concerns in mind. These schedules are not mandatory for pulp and paper manufacturers, but many consumers in developed countries now insist that their suppliers do abide by them. For example, many of the big publishing houses in Europe and North America demand that their paper supply originate from sustainable forests.

Even though the natural forests in Thailand are under great threat, most wood for industrial processing comes from plantations. The requirements regarding social performance make it difficult for Thai companies to comply with international conventions regarding sustainable forestry.

Many small farmers in Thailand see eucalyptus trees—used widely in the paper industry—as an economically attractive alternative to other cash crops such as tapioca or sugar cane, even though they have to be patient and wait for at least four years before the first 'harvesting.' But these farmers cannot make their plantations viable without having the whole family involved in the nurturing and maintenance of the trees, and they have poor understanding of the fact that child labour is prohibited by ILO conventions. When the time for harvesting the plantation trees arrives, the farmer can employ a contractor for the job and have the logs delivered to the wood processing factory. The work is carried out efficiently by the contractor, but the workers have very little influence on their conditions, and there are no possibilities to collectively negotiate with the company as stipulated by ILO conventions. The Thai attitude regarding organized labour is at odds with the international requirements, and this could be a serious obstacle for the country's wood processing industry, which has high ambitions to be an international player. Without an internationally recognized forestry certificate, it will be difficult to penetrate many markets.

The importance of networking in conducting a successful business is often emphasized in Western business philosophy. For a Thai, this goes without saying, but the networks are not the same as in the Western business world, where the primary reason for such relationships is the hope of making the acquaintance of people with technical competence which one lacks. In Thailand, the networks are of a more personal nature; it is more about keeping on the good side of influential people.

To conduct business successfully in Thailand, you have to establish contact within the country's power centres, namely the banking world, the military, and the civil service and government. A simple way to do this is by inviting representatives from these sectors onto the company board. Though government officials are excluded, a company can always find an army general (of whom there are many hundreds in Thailand) or a high banking official to become a member of the board. Through them, the company can obtain permits required to expand the business. Within government circles, you have to make informal contacts.

One day, the mill's production planning department asked me if we could make a special product for a Thai company. I investigated and came to the conclusion that we couldn't. Our production planner insisted. I protested that this would only result in the customer being disappointed with the quality of the eventual product. But the situation was that the company had already promised this special product. I wondered why we were so anxious to satisfy this customer's request. It turned out that the customer was a relative of a former minister of justice, and an old legal case our company was involved in would soon be heard before a higher court. Therefore we had to pull out all the stops to get the product

made. We made an effort but, as I had predicted, the goods weren't up to standard and were returned to us. We had, however, shown our goodwill by extending a favour to the client, and our company could, in return, expect some kind of reciprocation in the court.

The political landscape in Thailand is also dominated by businesspeople—many with very questionable ideals. All sorts of methods are used to obtain and maintain political power. Bribes paid to voters can be quite large. Others intimidate their political opponents or order subordinates to 'liquidate' their worst rivals. Before general elections in Thailand, sales of bullet-proof vests increase significantly, and security firms reap large profits. After many hardships and much financial investment on the road to power, there has to be some sort of dividend. Politicians give advantages to companies with whom they have an interest. When government tenders are put out for road building or school materials, the contracts go to companies affiliated with political figures.

Sometimes I miss the generosity in Western business relationships, where one cares about one's customers and takes care of them when they visit. In Thailand, people want to impress the visiting client rather than look after them. Dinners are arranged in elegant restaurants with exquisite dishes but, despite the wonderful hospitality, to some Westerners it can seem superficial.

Peter, who worked in our sales department, initially found it hard to get used to this different attitude towards customers. Serving coffee at internal company meetings had been stopped to cut costs. When Peter was visited by some potential foreign customers, he asked his secretary to bring coffee. Following what she thought was the new company policy, she returned with only a glass of water for each member of the delegation. Peter thought this was stingy and pushed to have the ban rescinded for important client visits. When the next delegation of clients arrived a week later, Peter ordered coffee and the secretary appeared with her tray—a cup of coffee for each of the visitors, and a glass of water for Peter.

Serving cold water is the normal practice in a Thai home when someone drops in for a chat. In the countryside, drinking coffee is still an exotic habit, and foreigners can get annoyed by the perceived poor treatment when visiting Thai friends: "We didn't even get a cup of coffee!" The Thai point of view is different: after being out in the sun, a cold glass of water is definitely more refreshing than a hot cup of coffee.

Serving a glass of water is a courtesy also practiced when you enter a tailor's shop or motorbike repair shop—in fact, many commercial places in Thailand. So, after all, it was not in any way meant to be impolite to serve iced water to foreign visitors.

As a supplier to a Thai company, one has to be prepared for the fact that the payment arrangements aren't as strict as in a Western country. If the supplier tries to charge penalty fees when the company doesn't pay bills on time, it is usually dismissed by the client as 'Western nonsense.' It is not until the supplier stops deliveries that the company

'finds' the invoices and promptly pays the remainder. Bureaucracy can also play a part in delaying the processing of invoices, and sometimes the CEO has to personally authorize the payment of a large sum, being the only one with the authority to do so. Any doubt about the quality of the delivered goods is also considered a valid reason by the receiving company to delay payment.

When the Thai banking world was in difficulties towards the close of the 1990s, many companies adopted the 'solution' of asking their suppliers to extend their credit period. In this way they virtually let the suppliers finance the company. One option for the suppliers was to terminate such business deals—but then face the very real risk of losing what they were owed. Redress through the legal system is limited. Thai legislation has not been very effective, and there isn't any working bankruptcy law to turn to when companies claim they don't have any money with which to pay their debts. The company can more or less ignore their debts and continue in business by simply changing their supplier.

The legislation for loan repayments is, however, very strict towards the individual. This can cause optimistic people to become victims. The repayments have to be kept up to date during the entire repayment period. This means that, even if there is only one repayment left, items can still be returned to the seller if the buyer is late in paying for them. When the good years in Thailand ended, many car buyers suddenly could no longer afford the repayments and had their cars repossessed. Of their previous repayments, they saw nothing.

Our company is planning to expand, with a new factory in China. They have been wise in recruiting a group of well-educated Chinese to staff the future plant, and a training programme will run for several years in the mill. I was entrusted to supervise one of the youngsters on the programme and was a bit surprised when he told me he had to work every Saturday, when the Thai staff only had to work every second Saturday. I got in touch with the personnel department and asked why. It turned out that the trainees were actually employed by the future Chinese company, and it was customary in China to work a six-day week. The Thai New Year celebration, Songkran, was the following week, and I asked whether the Chinese were meant to work through this, as well. Naturally, they were supposed to, as, in China, Songkran was not a holiday anyway. I then assumed that they should be free on the Chinese public holidays, but the personnel manager couldn't understand my position. The answer was no, of course: they were working in Thailand, and workers in Thailand didn't get time off on Chinese holidays. We never heard any protest from the Chinese trainees, since they were not spoiled with any extensive vacations at home, either.

There is a general atmosphere prevalent in a Thai workplace in which the stronger party controls a situation to his own advantage, without any legislation to act as a balancing force. The foreigner often experiences greed as a major factor in the Thai business environment. This can seem strange in a Buddhist society, where greed is supposed to be an underlying reason for life's sufferings. In such a different work environment, with special game rules, foreigners don't fit into the traditional pattern, and even if there is a well-defined organizational structure established by the CEO, they realize that the network in control of the company is an informal one. Foreigners easily get a feeling of being outsiders, and this can have a devastating effect for ambitious people.

☙❧

Some people say that Thais are individualistic and prefer to work by themselves rather than in teams. Many Thais willingly agree to this perception, and some even admit that this explains why the Thai national soccer team has difficulties competing internationally. When I ask young engineers in our company how they see their future and what expectations they have for their career path in the company, I often get the usual answer that one day they will resign and start their own little business.

Working together, on the other hand, *is* a true Thai virtue—and the social aspect at work is important. You very seldom find a Thai person working alone. Having friends and colleagues around can make work tolerable and fun at the same time. The Thai expressions for 'working' and to 'have a party' are also very similar, which reflects the emphasis most Thais give to being together for all sorts of reasons. Working hours, you preferably spend with friends, but what you actually accomplish is perhaps not the most important issue.

It may be easy to say that Thais cannot work in groups or succeed in joint efforts. This is not really the case, but for true accomplishments strong leadership is required. The consensus principle favoured in Western society is seldom found in successful working groups in Thailand. The team leader decides the objectives and targets for the team, and then has to find a way to get the team members committed to achieving the targets. The manager must create loyalty among his subordinates, and be able to provide something in exchange.

Now and then, the company considers salary increments, and the departmental managers are supposed to make proposals for senior management's consideration. Here is an opportunity to reward those who have performed well and have been loyal. Even though the departmental managers have limited authority, there are other ways to give favours and rewards to subordinates. Suppliers play an important role for a manufacturing company and are also a valuable source for unofficial benefits for employees. Seminars, study trips, and New Year gifts are offered in order to maintain good business relations, but it is the managers who hold the key to these fringe benefits, which they distribute to those to be awarded for their performance. With these tools, the departmental managers can exercise greater control over their teams.

I'm quite certain that the senior managers of Thai companies are well aware of these power plays, and this is why you seldom find any significant delegation of authority. Important decisions involving economic matters are taken by the top management, or by committees with members outside the control of the affected department. As a foreigner working in a Thai company, you may find it strange that, together with the responsibility entrusted to you, there is next to no authority. John, who is employed by the company as a production manager with focus on productivity improvements, soon found out that whatever he suggested regarding process modifications was submitted for review to a committee with representatives from other departments—before the proposal was presented to the management for approval. This procedure may seem humiliating to most professional foreigners in such a position, but it is a way for the top management to control supplier-receiver relations. The official policy is that there is no need for any authority at the lower level because the 'team' makes all decisions.

I have found the purpose of many Thai committees different from my earlier Scandinavian experiences. The committee members don't come together with the same intention—to come to a common understanding—but rather to control what is suggested by other departments. This may develop into a delicate balancing act for the managers participating in the committee meetings. To get your proposals accepted by the committee, you must have the support of other delegates, and this can be obtained by endorsing the ideas and projects of others. The committee function develops to a state where the managers become mutually dependent on each other and the control function is lost.

I sometimes feel a kinship with the main character in James Clavell's novel, *Shogun*. The English sea captain, John Blackthorne, finds himself in a dramatic, internal political power struggle after a shipwreck on the Japanese coast in the early 1600s. The stranded commander doesn't understand much of the intrigue that surrounds him. Instead he is used as a political pawn in the ensuing drama. He has a dream to return to England, and eventually gets permission to build another ship. One night, when the ship is almost completed, it is destroyed by fire for some unknown reason. His Japanese protector tries to comfort him by saying that they will build a new ship, but, at the same time, the reader realizes that the captain will never leave Japan.

21. At Home In Thailand

What is it that makes so many foreigners stay on, year after year, in Thailand? Sure, there are many practical difficulties for a Westerner living and working in Thai society, where the underlying values are not so clear. For most people, however, living in Thailand is an exciting experience, where every day offers something unexpected. For an open-minded foreigner it is a continuous learning process, where you develop your understanding of human relations.

Thailand is often referred to as the Land of Smiles, and this can mean much more than just a facial expression. Westerners in Thailand are met with a friendliness that is seldom found elsewhere in the world. The pace of life, especially in the countryside, is more relaxing, and people still have time for each other—and this also includes foreigners. These values have to some extent been lost in the Western world, and Thailand offers a haven for foreigners who want to participate in a different society.

Those foreigners who live and work officially in Thailand got their work permit because of their professional competence. In spite of all the difficulties found in the workplace, many long-term residents still feel that they are participating in a development that feels meaningful and challenging. In spite of the economic crisis in Southeast Asia, there is a strong belief in a better future. This feeling is contagious even for foreigners who have dared to permanently leave the safe environment of their home country behind them.

So what happened to the two ignorant Swedes who challenged the opinion of their friends and families at home and moved to this exotic country so far away? Well, we are still living in Thailand and have managed to overcome most of the difficulties we experienced in the beginning. Or maybe we have just got accustomed to the circumstances that, from a Swedish horizon, seemed so strange. After some years, we realized that we must try to live according to local customs and not fight everything that did not conform to our Western values.

Living in a fenced residential compound with the continuous roar from the factories in the background was not an environment that really made us feel at home in Thailand. It was convenient with the mill only ten minutes drive away and the market within walking distance, but after five years we missed a true home, where we could relax the way we were used to. We started to think of alternatives, but being a foreigner can make life complicated in Thailand. As a foreigner you are not allowed to buy land. Of course, there are solutions to these kinds of obstacles, and Thai lawyers willingly assist with suitable arrangements.

Still, the idea of making Thailand our second home grew in our minds, and we began to investigate how to make this possible. From the very beginning, we were intrigued by traditional wooden Thai houses. We visited some inspiring homes and bought books on this topic. Could we create something that would compensate for the red wooden cottage that we had left in the forests of Sweden? After lengthy discussions, sketches began to take shape in my notebook. We wanted to combine comfortable Western living with the charming appearance of the Thai traditional wooden house. Finally we decided to go ahead, and we discussed the issue with our friend, Khun Yaa. "No problem," he said with a smile. "You can lease a piece of land from my parents in a small farming village not too far away from the factory." One rainy day he went with us to see his parents and the proposed site next to their house. We drove along the main highway and turned into a local road, passing a small town before entering a bumpy, narrow road. The road wound between rice paddies and tapioca fields, and we had difficulty negotiating all the potholes. We started to hesitate. Where were we going? We passed houses embedded between mango trees, and a small village with a twinkling temple. The rain itensified and the landscape did not look very inviting. Suddenly Khun Yaa stopped in front of a house close to the road.

His mother and father came out and greeted us with respectful *wais*. The plot of land our friend had in mind was an old mango orchard, now untended, with banana plants gradually taking over. The rain fell even harder and the ground rapidly became very muddy when we walked around. It was far from romantic, and it was difficult to visualize our house in this environment. Then I looked into Khun Yaa's face and saw a big smile. This was the place where he had grown up and where

his parents were still living, and he was delighted that we, a foreign couple, would consider his home as our future home, too. We did not immediately make up our minds, but gradually we realized that this would be a very practical arrangement.

But to whom could we entrust the building of our new home? Some time before, we had seen an exhibition and sales area where a local company had built some wooden Thai houses in various styles. We stopped by and enquired about the possibility of building a house according to our own specifications. The sales agent, Khun Prayad, was very courteous and did not see any difficulties in making a customized house for us. The house would be prefabricated in northern Thailand from second-hand wood and delivered in sections to Khun Yaa's land for final erection. The next week, we returned to Khun Prayad with our drawings and signed a contract.

The design was similar to the traditional styles we had seen, with the house built on poles, leaving an open space underneath. Khun Prayad would be responsible for the wooden construction, and we would take care of the foundation work and the kitchen area and bathroom to be built on the ground floor. Now we had to find craftsmen to help us with the other parts of our project. In the village, there were people with various skills. Khun Wee was very good at concrete work, and Khun Chit was good with electrical installations. In Bangkok, a sub-contractor was assigned for the complete installation of a Western kitchen and bathroom. Everything was now on track.

Soon the building site was cleared, and the foundations for the big poles, which are the backbone of a Thai house, were prepared. The villagers took great interest in our project, and we eagerly awaited the arrival of the wood sections from northern Thailand. One day, three big trucks turned up with a team of construction workers, and they started to unload the different sections for the house. It was time to prepare for the pole raising ceremony, much anticipated by the villagers. The following day, we gathered at the site, and one of the poles was decorated with banana leaves and a miniature bamboo fishing trap, where we put a banknote. Incense sticks were lit, and the oldest man in the village, with his hands placed in a respectful *wai*, solemnly asked the spirit of the site to protect the house. The first pole was carried to the foundation hole, raised and fixed in position, then some others followed with supporting beams attached. We could almost visualize the finished house in front of us. What a wonderful feeling.

No Thai gathering is complete without food and drink, and our neighbour had been preparing a feast the whole morning. We gathered in the shade of some big mango trees and soon everyone was enjoying the dishes laid out for the occasion. I sat with my bowl filled with rice on my knee and my beer beside me, looking at the set of thick wooden poles pointing skyward. Something was wrong. I looked again at the notches where the beams for the second floor would be attached. Were they too low to ground? Surely I hadn't drunk too much already. I left my bowl on the ground and went to take a closer look. The notches in the poles were at the same level as my shoulders—but we were going to build the kitchen and bathroom on the ground floor. I called for Khun Prayad and asked him about this alarming deviation from our agreed plans. Well, he said, they had had difficulties finding poles of sufficient length, so the second floor had to be 1.5 metres above the ground rather than the 2.5 specified in the drawing. In a situation like this, you have to control yourself and keep cool. *Jai yen*, as they say in Thailand. With the assistance of Khun Yaa, we managed to persuade the building company to return everything—poles, panels, the whole lot—and deliver a new batch of material according to what we had originally agreed upon.

Two months later, the new materials arrived, and the construction of the house made good progress. Because of this initial delay, we were

now entering the rainy season, and we had good opportunities to test the teakwood-tile roof. Water was dripping through in different places, and the supervisor instructed his workers to add silicon sealant between the tiles where he assumed that the water was leaking through. I tried to convince Khun Prayad that this could not be the correct way to make a waterproof roof, but he insisted. After a number of discussions about the condition of the roof, Khun Prayad finally told me that, when living in Thailand, I had to accept some rain leakage. He obviously wanted to finish the job as soon as possible and collect his fee, but we managed to make a deal. I accepted the construction with a deduction of the original price, and later asked some local workers to partly re-do the roof.

In the meantime, Khun Wee had started his work casting the concrete underneath the building, but he was a little confused about the notion of walls for the kitchen area. Why did we need walls when we had a wonderful large space with good shelter from the sun and rain. This would be an excellent place for cooking. Walls would only make it uncomfortably hot and not allow the chilli fumes to escape from the pans. The area we had suggested for the kitchen was quite small, and there wouldn't be much space for many people to sit on the floor and assist with the cooking. We insisted on our Western style kitchen, and soon the Bangkok company arrived with the material for the kitchen surfaces and cupboards, which were made to size on site. The neighbours were curious about our stainless-steel sinks and gas stove set into the wooden worktop, but they felt sorry for Gunilla, who had to stand up all the time when cooking. There was hardly any space on the floor for her to sit on.

Our house required a power supply far beyond what is normal for a Thai house in the countryside. In addition to some fluorescent tubes, most houses are only equipped with a refrigerator, a rice cooker, and a TV set, and a ten-amp main fuse is enough. We started to calculate the power demand for our house: two AC units, two water heaters for the showers, an electric baking oven, freezer, refrigerator, etcetera. All together we estimated our requirements for electrical power, with some margin for future expansions, to be fifty amps. When we visited the district office to apply for the electrical connection, the officer almost jumped out of his skin when he saw our application. "Are you going to start a factory?" he asked in dismay.

Khun Chit could now start his wiring work, but soon I got a little suspicious about his competence. The installation in our house was obviously greater than anything he had taken on before. Even with my limited experience of electrical installations, the dimensions of the cables didn't seem to match the equipment they were supposed to supply. How would a main breaker with a designed current of ten amps service a five-kilowatt baking oven? "No problem, we just put an extra twenty-amp breaker next to the oven."

I consulted the electrical manager at the mill, and he promised to help me with a safe installation. He went with me to the house and had a very diplomatic discussion with Khun Chit, who unwillingly had to agree to supervision of his work by one of the factory electricians.

One hurdle after another was eventually overcome and we soon filled the house with things that make life comfortable for a foreigner: tables, chairs, beds, and curtains around the windows. At last we were ready for our first night in the house, our dreams come true. After sunset, the village is almost completely dark, with the exception of some weak fluorescent tubes in Khun Yaa's parents' house behind the mango trees. That first night, the sky was clear and we were sitting on the verandah gazing at the constellations that looked different from those we were used to in Sweden. Crickets and cicadas filled the night air with their screeching. Now and then a car passed by on the road, and some dogs howled in the dark. We went to bed with a feeling of starting a new life.

We hadn't slept long before the roosters in the village started their night chorus. One after the other they tried their best to out-do their companions in volume. We didn't get much more sleep, and by dawn, when the roosters had performed their duties, a new and terrible noise filled the environment. It was the morning delivery truck, which arrived in the village with fresh vegetables. On top of the roof of the old pick-up truck was a giant loudspeaker blasting out Thai pop music in the early morning hours. I suppose that this was an effective way to attract customers from the village houses, where people were gradually getting to their feet. For us, not used to this type of nightlife, this was not the relaxing upcountry environment we had expected. Before long we got accustomed to these all-night sounds, and found both the roosters and the morning pop concert quite comforting.

The news about our house spread rapidly among our friends in Sweden, who asked about the possibility of visiting us in our new Thai home. This development had not been in our plans. We had only intended this to

be a weekend hide-away from the factory environment. The traditional
Thai house normally consists of a cluster of buildings round an open
courtyard, and I looked into the idea of attaching another building to
the first one. Eventually I came up with an unconventional solution that
still maintained Thai features. The construction company had left a bad
taste in our mouths, so we had to find some trustworthy people to help
us with stage two in our house project. Khun Yaa has many cousins with
various skills, and one of them was an experienced carpenter.

With some hesitation we hired Khun Daeng to build our guesthouse,
and he brought together some other people from the village to assist
him. Poles, beams, and planks soon arrived in front of our house, and
Khun Daeng checked every piece before acceptance. Only perfect
material was allowed. The building team started early in the mornings
and, without any construction drawings, they erected the frame for the
house. We could see that this was not the first house Khun Daeng had
built. He seemed to have all the necessary design features in his head.
The whole team seemed to enjoy the job, and would work more or less
the whole day with only a short break for lunch. Not until the sun started
to disappear behind the horizon did they collect their tools and sit down
together to admire their accomplishments for the day.

It was a pleasure watching the construction work from our verandah. It was obvious that the team wanted to make a well-built house. They took pride in their work and were determined to do a better job than the big construction company from the city. Khun Daeng and his crew were having so much fun, they asked us whether they could work also on Sundays. As we were usually at the main house over the weekends, they would try not to make so much noise. In just two months, the beautiful Thai-style cottage was completed next to the main house, and it was a very proud team that posed for pictures in front of it when Khun Daeng announced that all was ready.

To start with, we were a little worried about whether we would be accepted in this rural environment, but by having the local people build our house, we became members of the local community. We had entrusted our project to them and provided work opportunities. In return, they had given their best and were happy with what they had accomplished—and delighted that we were very pleased with their work. We were met with a friendliness that made us feel welcome from the very first day. Now we were ready to welcome family members and friends to experience the Thai countryside with us.

☙❦❧

With our acceptance in the local community, we were also expected to contribute to and participate in the local social life. Our village has its own football team of teenage boys. Khun Yaa is the enthusiastic coach, even if he is not as fit as he used to be. There aren't many other activities in the village for these boys, and, besides the fun of playing, the team has an important social function.

During the cool season, tournaments are arranged between the villages in the district, and the evening practice on the football field beside the school intensifies. It's a pleasure to watch the boys running on the dusty pitch chasing the ball in the hot sun. Some of them wear football boots; some run barefoot. But there are some expenses involved with participating in a tournament. A fee has to be paid, and the boys must have proper strips with the name of the team printed on the back. A sponsor has to be found, and fortunately there is one foreigner in the village. We have, over time, provided many sets of football kits, as well as fancy trophies for the winning teams. As a sponsor, you are expected to attend the tournaments and watch the matches sitting on a sofa under a canopy, together with representatives from the local community. We also present the trophies to the winning team and the runners-up. It's a great honour for the team captain to receive the trophy and take it back to the village, where they celebrate with a big party.

After supporting the village team for some time, Khun Yaa asked me whether it would be possible to use our family name for the football team. The boys, he said, would be very proud of having our family name on the back of their shirts. And so 'Team Kolmodin' appeared in the local tournaments—and they were quite successful. Before long, Team Kolmodin was reaching finals and winning trophies. From the loudspeakers by the side of the football field, located between the school and the temple, the name Kolmodin was repeatedly announced during the matches, and the team became renowned in the district.

After the first tournament success, the team expressed their gratitude to me, the sponsor, and I was completely taken by surprise when Khun Yaa presented me with the trophy. He told me that the team would be happy if I would like to keep it in our house. I was part of their success and, with my sponsorship and attendance at the matches, I had motivated them to do their best on the field. For them it was completely natural to give the trophy to me. I felt deeply honoured, and space had to be made on the bookshelf in our living room.

One fancy trophy after another soon lined up beside the first, and over the years the trophies themselves also grew bigger, so that we had to put them on the floor. Eventually our living room looked like the boardroom of Real Madrid. What should we do with all these trophies? The King of Thailand faces the same situation with awards won by Thai athletes in international competitions. When Thai Olympic medallists return after a successful games, they are granted an audience with the King, where, in gratitude for his patronage, they present their medals to him. In the grounds of the Grand Palace in Bangkok, many of these are on display in a museum. Maybe we will have to arrange a village museum quite soon.

☙❧

But there was still one important task to undertake with the house after it had been completed: a ceremony to have our home blessed by the monks from the temple in the village. This was an event that had to be properly celebrated, and Khun Yaa and his family were happy to assist with all the arrangements for the big day. The monks were consulted regarding a suitable day for the ceremony, and invitations were sent out to villagers and friends. Helping hands were easily obtained from the village. Women prepared food, tables and chairs were borrowed from the temple, strings of lamps were arranged between the trees in front of the house, and an amplifier with big loudspeakers was installed for the entertainment. There was going to be a party, and it was out of our hands.

On the morning of the auspicious day, nine monks arrived from the temple. They sat in a line next to each other on the floor in our TV room, which we had cleared of all furniture. A long cotton string was looped around the house, passing through the hands of the monks, and ending up at a Buddha image on a small stool. Gunilla and I, together with our children, who had arrived for the occasion (it was Christmas time, also), sat down along the opposite wall facing the solemn-looking monks. The villagers filled all the available space around. The monks started to chant mantras, and the smoke from the incense sticks filled every corner of the house. With our crossed legs we soon found it uncomfortable sitting on the floor, but at last the chanting ended and the monks were treated to a feast of various dishes, which we brought forward to them. Now we could see smiles in the faces of the monks, who took no offence at our clumsy manners in serving them. Once the monks had eaten, everyone then joined in and had their share of the many dishes set out on the floor mats.

After the meal, the senior monk had to perform the important task of putting some sacred and secret symbols above the doors—in order to dismiss all evil spirits from disturbing the residents of the house. The bowl of water that had been standing beside the monks during the ceremony was carried around, and with a bunch of sticks, the monk sprinkled the blessed water on the house and all the guests. After fulfilling their obligations, the monks went back to the temple, and we felt that we had been properly integrated into the Thai community.

After a while, more guests started to arrive for the big house-warming party in front of the house. Multicoloured lamps illuminated the garden and Thai pop music filled the air. Beer and whiskey bottles were spread out on the tables, and soon the party was in full swing. Our building team had arranged a small stage, and Gunilla had invited a group of children to entertain us with classical music and dances. Dishes were continuously brought from the cooking area and put on the tables. The villagers were a little shy and not fully comfortable mingling with our friends from the mill and Gunilla's school, but they still enjoyed the party in the background.

A party never lasts forever, and at the end of the night Gunilla and I were the last ones left standing in front of our house.

Our Thai home.

All You Want to Know About Thailand, from
ASIA BOOKS

Bridging the Gap:
Managing the Cross-Cultural Workplace in Thailand
By Kriengsak Niratpattanasai

Bridging the Gap is a practical and entertaining guide to help foreign and Thai businesspeople working together in Thailand. The book is divided into four sections, starting with an insightful account of the Thai cultural make-up, and a revealing study on how Thais regard foreigners in the workplace, and vice versa. Real-life case studies highlight common misunderstandings and offer solutions for awkward situations. Also includes a section on how to handle official social functions such as weddings and funerals.

The Essential Guide for Anyone Who Works,
or Does Business, In Thailand

Managing the Cross-Cultural Workplace in Thailand

BRIDGING
THE
GAP

"Essential reading for anybody who wants to do business in Thailand.
It shall stand as a reference for future generations."
– Frank-Jurgen Richter, World Economic Forum.

KRIENGSAK NIRATPATTANASAI

Mai Pen Rai Means Never Mind
By Carol Hollinger

Carol Hollinger was a housewife, mother, and teacher, and *Mai Pen Rai* is her humorous, often hilarious account of her experience in all those roles during her stay in Thailand, where her husband was stationed in the US foreign service. A brilliant observer of customs, manners, and cultural differences, she writes frankly and unsparingly of herself and her fellow Americans, and relates both the fun and the frustration of communicating with Thai people—without being coy or condescending.

A Classic Book, Not Only For All Foreign Residents and Visitors, but Also for Thais Themselves.

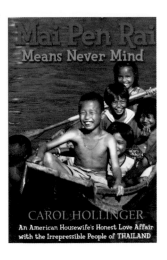

Learning Thai: Just Enough to Get By and More
By Warankna Tuwayanonde & Paul Wallis

A phrase book and guide for you to learn and understand Thai in a simple and comprehensive way. With this book you won't need a Thai teacher. When in doubt, just ask any Thai. Includes the necessary keys to the language, and examples of dialogue in Thai to help familiarize you with the Thai way of speaking.

Pronunciation. Grammar. Useful Words and Phrases for Travellers and Expats. Organized by Subject: (Shopping, Transport, Hotels, etc). Mini Dictionary.

Bangkok People
By James Eckardt

"The killing starts around 8 p.m. and can go on till the very early hours." The pig butcher.

"Flying off to the Bahamas one day, Paris the next." The TV producer.

From business tycoons, bargirls, and bodysnatchers to street vendors, slum-dwellers, socialites and singers, *Bangkok People* takes the reader into the daily lives of city denizens—both Thai and expat, and from the filthy rich to the just plain filthy. This fascinating, funny, sometimes serious and occasionally odd collection plunges right into the heart of the myriad masses who make this mad metropolis tick.

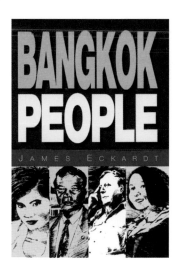